**Kaplan** ~~Publishing are constantly finding new~~ ly fi
ways to ~~make a difference to your s~~ ur s
exciting online resources really do ~~offer something~~
different to students looking for exam success.

This book comes with free MyKaplan online resources so that you can study anytime, anywhere. **This free online resource is not sold separately and is included in the price of the book.**

Having purchased this book, you have access to the following online study materials:

| CONTENT | AAT | |
|---|---|---|
| | Text | Kit |
| Electronic version of the book | ✓ | ✓ |
| Progress tests with instant answers | ✓ | |
| Mock assessments online | ✓ | ✓ |
| Material updates | ✓ | ✓ |

### How to access your online resources

Kaplan Financial students will already have a MyKaplan account and these extra resources will be available to you online. You do not need to register again, as this process was completed when you enrolled. If you are having problems accessing online materials, please ask your course administrator.

If you are not studying with Kaplan and did not purchase your book via a Kaplan website, to unlock your extra online resources please go to www.mykaplan.co.uk/addabook (even if you have set up an account and registered books previously). You will then need to enter the ISBN number (on the title page and back cover) and the unique pass key number contained in the scratch panel below to gain access. You will also be required to enter additional information during this process to set up or confirm your account details.

If you purchased through Kaplan Flexible Learning or via the Kaplan Publishing website you will automatically receive an e-mail invitation to MyKaplan. Please register your details using this email to gain access to your content. If you do not receive the e-mail or book content, please contact Kaplan Publishing.

### Your Code and Information

This code can only be used once for the registration of one book online. This registration and your online content will expire when the final sittings for the examinations covered by this book have taken place. Please allow one hour from the time you submit your book details for us to process your request.

Please scratch the film to access your MyKaplan code.

Please be aware that this code is case-sensitive and you will need to include the dashes within the passcode, but not when entering the ISBN. For further technical support, please visit www.MyKaplan.co.uk

**Standard Loan**

rthyr Tydf'

72621

# AAT

# AQ2016

---

## Bookkeeping Controls

---

# EXAM KIT

This Exam Kit supports study for the following AAT qualifications:

AAT Foundation Certificate in Accounting – Level 2
AAT Foundation Diploma in Accounting and Business – Level 2
AAT Foundation Certificate in Bookkeeping – Level 2
AAT Foundation Award in Accounting Software – Level 2
AAT Level 2 Award in Accounting Skills to Run Your Business
AAT Foundation Certificate in Accounting at SCQF Level 5

**British Library Cataloguing-in-Publication Data**

A catalogue record for this book is available from the British Library.

Published by:

Kaplan Publishing UK
Unit 2 The Business Centre
Molly Millar's Lane
Wokingham
Berkshire
RG41 2QZ

ISBN: 978-1-78740-524-0

© Kaplan Financial Limited, 2019

Printed and bound in Great Britain.

# CONTENTS

---

**Features in this exam kit**

In addition to providing a wide ranging bank of real exam style questions, we have also included in this kit:

- unit-specific information and advice on exam technique

- our recommended approach to make your revision for this particular unit as effective as possible.

---

You will find a wealth of other resources to help you with your studies on the AAT website:

www.aat.org.uk/

Quality and accuracy are of the utmost importance to us so if you spot an error in any of our products, please send an email to mykaplanreporting@kaplan.com with full details, or follow the link to the feedback form in MyKaplan.

Our Quality Co-ordinator will work with our technical team to verify the error and take action to ensure it is corrected in future editions.

# UNIT-SPECIFIC INFORMATION

## THE EXAM

### FORMAT OF THE ASSESSMENT

The assessment will comprise ten independent tasks. Students will be assessed by computer-based assessment.

In any one assessment, students may not be assessed on all content, or on the full depth or breadth of a piece of content. The content assessed may change over time to ensure validity of assessment, but all assessment criteria will be tested over time.

The learning outcomes for this unit are as follows:

| | Learning outcome | Weighting |
|---|---|---|
| 1 | Understand payment methods | 5% |
| 2 | Understand controls in a bookkeeping system | 5% |
| 3 | Use control accounts | 20% |
| 4 | Use the journal | 50% |
| 5 | Reconcile a bank statement with the cash book | 20% |
| | Total | 100% |

**Time allowed**

1½ hours

### PASS MARK

The pass mark for all AAT CBAs is 70%.

**Always keep your eye on the clock and make sure you attempt all questions!**

## DETAILED SYLLABUS

The detailed syllabus and study guide written by the AAT can be found at:

www.aat.org.uk/

# INDEX TO QUESTIONS AND ANSWERS

# EXAM TECHNIQUE

- **Do not skip any of the material** in the syllabus.

- **Read each question** *very* carefully.

- **Double-check your answer** before committing yourself to it.

- Answer **every** question – if you do not know an answer to a multiple choice question or true/false question, you don't lose anything by guessing. Think carefully before you **guess**.

- If you are answering a multiple-choice question, **eliminate first those answers that you know are wrong.** Then choose the most appropriate answer from those that are left.

- **Don't panic** if you realise you've answered a question incorrectly. Getting one question wrong will not mean the difference between passing and failing.

## Computer-based assessments (CBA) – tips

- Do not attempt a CBA until you have **completed all study material** relating to it.

- On the AAT website there is a CBA demonstration. It is **ESSENTIAL** that you attempt this before your real CBA. You will become familiar with how to move around the CBA screens and the way that questions are formatted, increasing your confidence and speed in the actual exam.

- Be sure you understand how to use the **software** before you start the exam. If in doubt, ask the assessment centre staff to explain it to you.

- Questions are **displayed on the screen** and answers are entered using keyboard and mouse. At the end of the exam, you are given a certificate showing the result you have achieved.

- In addition to the traditional multiple-choice question type, CBAs will also contain **other types of questions**, such as number-entry questions, drag and drop, true/false, pick lists or drop down menus or hybrids of these.

- In some CBAs you will have to type in complete computations or written answers.

- You need to be sure you **know how to answer questions** of this type before you sit the exam, through practice.

# KAPLAN'S RECOMMENDED REVISION APPROACH

## QUESTION PRACTICE IS THE KEY TO SUCCESS

Success in professional examinations relies upon you acquiring a firm grasp of the required knowledge at the tuition phase. In order to be able to do the questions, knowledge is essential.

However, the difference between success and failure often hinges on your exam technique on the day and making the most of the revision phase of your studies.

The **Kaplan Study Text** is the starting point, designed to provide the underpinning knowledge to tackle all questions. However, in the revision phase, poring over text books is not the answer.

**Kaplan Pocket Notes** are designed to help you quickly revise a topic area; however you then need to practise questions. There is a need to progress to exam style questions as soon as possible, and to tie your exam technique and technical knowledge together.

**The importance of question practice cannot be over-emphasised.**

The recommended approach below is designed by expert tutors in the field, in conjunction with their knowledge of the examiner and the specimen assessment.

**You need to practise as many questions as possible in the time you have left.**

## OUR AIM

Our aim is to get you to the stage where you can attempt exam questions confidently, to time, in a closed book environment, with no supplementary help (i.e. to simulate the real examination experience).

Practising your exam technique is also vitally important for you to assess your progress and identify areas of weakness that may need more attention in the final run up to the examination.

In order to achieve this we recognise that initially you may feel the need to practice some questions with open book help.

**Good exam technique is vital.**

# THE KAPLAN REVISION PLAN

## Stage 1: Assess areas of strengths and weaknesses

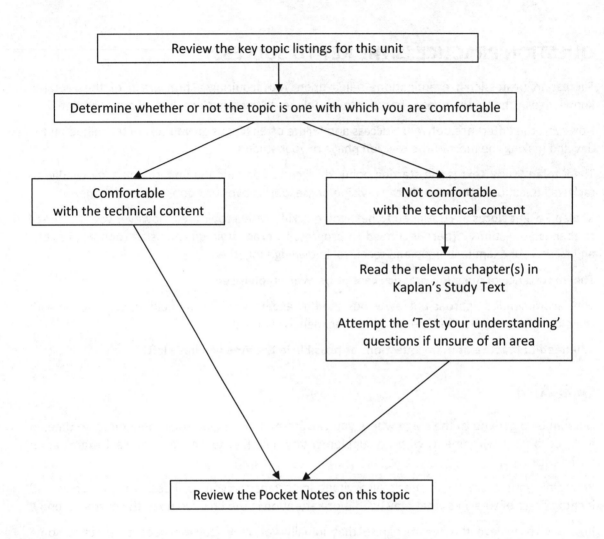

## Stage 2: Practise questions

Follow the order of revision of topics as presented in this Kit and attempt the questions in the order suggested.

Try to avoid referring to Study Texts and your notes and the model answer until you have completed your attempt.

Review your attempt with the model answer and assess how much of the answer you achieved.

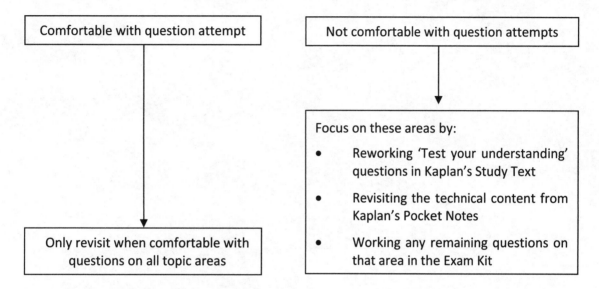

## Stage 3: Final pre-exam revision

We recommend that you **attempt at least one mock examination** containing a set of previously unseen exam-standard questions.

Attempt the mock CBA online in timed, closed book conditions to simulate the real exam experience.

# Section 1

# PRACTICE QUESTIONS

## THE JOURNAL

**1    INTREPID INTERIORS**

(a)    Intrepid Interiors has started a new business, Intrepid Exteriors, and a new set of accounts are to be opened.  A partially completed journal to record the opening entries is shown below.

**Record the journal entries needed in the accounts in the general ledger of Intrepid Exteriors to deal with the opening entries.**

| Account name | Amount £ | Debit ✓ | Credit ✓ |
|---|---|---|---|
| Cash at bank | 7,250 | | |
| Bank loan | 5,000 | | |
| Capital | 10,625 | | |
| Motor vehicles | 4,750 | | |
| Insurances | 575 | | |
| Stationery | 300 | | |
| Sundry expenses | 225 | | |
| Motor expenses | 135 | | |
| Advertising | 990 | | |
| Rent and rates | 1,400 | | |
| Journal to record the opening entries of new business | | | |

(b)    **From the list below, select which one of the following transactions would be recorded in the journal.**

|  |
|---|
|  |

Picklist: Credit sale, contra, electricity expense, reimbursement of petty cash

## 2 BEDROOM BITS

(a) Record the journal entries needed in the accounts in the general ledger of Bedroom Bits to show if each item is a debit or credit.

| Account name | Amount £ | Debit ✓ | Credit ✓ |
|---|---|---|---|
| Cash | 325 | | |
| Cash at bank | 9,625 | | |
| Capital | 22,008 | | |
| Fixtures and fittings | 4,250 | | |
| Insurance | 1,050 | | |
| Loan from bank | 15,000 | | |
| Miscellaneous expenses | 413 | | |
| Motor vehicle | 19,745 | | |
| Office expenses | 350 | | |
| Rent and rates | 1,250 | | |

(b) From the list below, select which one of the following transactions would be recorded in the journal.

| |
|---|
| |

Picklist: Prompt payment discount given, the return of goods to a supplier, interest received from the bank, irrecoverable debt written off

## 3 GARDEN GATES

Record the journal entries in the general ledger of Garden Gates to show if each item is a debit or a credit

| Account name | Amount £ | Debit ✓ | Credit ✓ |
|---|---|---|---|
| Cash | 450 | | |
| Cash at bank | 11,125 | | |
| Capital | 26,248 | | |
| Plant and machinery | 5,050 | | |
| Insurance | 990 | | |
| Loan from bank | 12,500 | | |
| General office expenses | 378 | | |
| Motor vehicle | 20,755 | | |

# PAYROLL

4   **IVANO**

Ivano's pay details for June are listed below:

| Transaction | Amount £ |
|---|---|
| Gross pay | 2,400 |
| PAYE | 480 |
| Employee's NIC | 245 |
| Employee's contribution to pension | 80 |
| Employer's NIC | 255 |

**Fill in the boxes required below:**

(a)

|  | Amount £ |
|---|---|
| Net pay |  |

(b)

|  | Amount £ |
|---|---|
| Wages and salaries (Employer's expense) |  |

(c)

|  | Amount £ |
|---|---|
| Liabilities (HMRC and pension) |  |

5   **ANNA**

Anna's pay details for June are listed below:

| Transaction | Amount £ |
|---|---|
| Gross pay | 1,400 |
| PAYE | 280 |
| Employee's NIC | 125 |
| Employer's contribution to pension | 70 |
| Employee's contribution to pension | 60 |
| Employer's NIC | 135 |

**Fill in the boxes required below:**

**(a)**

|  | Amount £ |
|---|---|
| Net pay |  |

**(b)**

|  | Amount £ |
|---|---|
| Wages and salaries (Employer's expense) |  |

**(c)**

|  | Amount £ |
|---|---|
| Liabilities (HMRC and pension) |  |

## 6 GROSS PAY 1

Which of the items listed below would be added to an employee's gross pay to calculate the total wages expense?

| Item | Added to gross pay ✓ | Not added to gross pay ✓ |
|---|---|---|
| Trade Union subscription |  |  |
| Employer's NIC |  |  |
| Employee's Pension |  |  |
| Employer's Pension |  |  |
| Employee's NIC |  |  |

## 7 GROSS PAY 2

Which of the items listed below would be deducted from an employee's gross pay to calculate net pay?

| Item | Deducted from gross pay ✓ | Not deducted from gross pay ✓ |
|---|---|---|
| Employer's NIC |  |  |
| Commission |  |  |
| Employee's NIC |  |  |
| Employee pension contribution |  |  |
| PAYE |  |  |

**8    A POCKET FULL OF POSES**

A Pocket Full of Poses pays its employees by cheque every month and maintains a wages control account.  A summary of last month's payroll transactions is shown below:

| Item | £ |
|---|---|
| Gross wages | 15,000 |
| Employers' NI | 1,755 |
| Employees' NI | 1,410 |
| Income tax | 4,335 |
| Employers' pension contributions | 1,000 |
| Employees' pension contributions | 850 |

**Record the journal entries needed in the general ledger to:**

**(i)     Record the wages expense**

**(ii)    Record the HMRC liability**

**(iii)   Record the net wages paid to the employees**

**(iv)   Record the pension liability.**

(i)

| Account name | Amount £ | Debit ✓ | Credit ✓ |
|---|---|---|---|
|  |  |  |  |
|  |  |  |  |

(ii)

| Account name | Amount £ | Debit ✓ | Credit ✓ |
|---|---|---|---|
|  |  |  |  |
|  |  |  |  |

(iii)

| Account name | Amount £ | Debit ✓ | Credit ✓ |
|---|---|---|---|
|  |  |  |  |
|  |  |  |  |

(iv)

| Account name | Amount £ | Debit ✓ | Credit ✓ |
|---|---|---|---|
|  |  |  |  |
|  |  |  |  |

Picklist for each: Bank, Employees NI, Employers NI, HMRC, Income tax, Net wages, Pension, Trade union, Wages control, Wages expense.

## 9 RHYME TIME

Rhyme Time pays its employees by cheque every month and maintains a wages control account. A summary of last month's payroll transactions is shown below:

| Item | £ |
|---|---|
| Gross wages | 10,130 |
| Employers' NI | 1,185 |
| Employees' NI | 1,006 |
| Income tax | 2,835 |
| Employers' pension contributions | 600 |
| Employees' pension contributions | 550 |

**Record the journal entries needed in the general ledger to:**

**(i)    Record the wages expense**

**(ii)   Record the HMRC liability**

**(iii)  Record the net wages paid to the employees**

**(iv)   Record the pension liability.**

(i)

| Account name | Amount £ | Debit ✓ | Credit ✓ |
|---|---|---|---|
|  |  |  |  |
|  |  |  |  |

(ii)

| Account name | Amount £ | Debit ✓ | Credit ✓ |
|---|---|---|---|
|  |  |  |  |
|  |  |  |  |

(iii)

| Account name | Amount £ | Debit ✓ | Credit ✓ |
|---|---|---|---|
|  |  |  |  |
|  |  |  |  |

(iv)

| Account name | Amount £ | Debit ✓ | Credit ✓ |
|---|---|---|---|
|  |  |  |  |
|  |  |  |  |

## 10   DOWN & OUT

Down & Out pays it employees by cheque every month and maintains a wages control account.  A summary of last month's payroll transactions is shown below:

| Item | £ |
|---|---|
| Gross wages | 8,542 |
| Employers' NI | 1,025 |
| Employees' NI | 940 |
| Income tax | 1,708 |
| Trade union fees | 425 |

**Record the journal entries needed in the general ledger to:**

**(i)     Record the wages expense**

**(ii)    Record the HMRC liability**

**(iii)   Record the net wages paid to the employees**

**(iv)   Record the trade union liability.**

(i)

| Account name | Amount £ | Debit ✓ | Credit ✓ |
|---|---|---|---|
|  |  |  |  |
|  |  |  |  |

(ii)

| Account name | Amount £ | Debit ✓ | Credit ✓ |
|---|---|---|---|
|  |  |  |  |
|  |  |  |  |

(iii)

| Account name | Amount £ | Debit ✓ | Credit ✓ |
|---|---|---|---|
|  |  |  |  |
|  |  |  |  |

(iv)

| Account name | Amount £ | Debit ✓ | Credit ✓ |
|---|---|---|---|
|  |  |  |  |
|  |  |  |  |

Picklist for each: Bank, Employees NI, Employers NI, HMRC, Income Tax, Net wages, Trade union, Wages control, Wages expense.

**11    DEV**

Dev pays its employees by cheque every month and maintains a wages control account.  A summary of last month's payroll transactions is shown below:

| Item | £ |
|---|---|
| Gross wages | 12,500 |
| Employers' NI | 1,463 |
| Employees' NI | 1,175 |
| Income tax | 3,613 |
| Trade union fees | 500 |

**Record the journal entries needed in the general ledger to:**

**(i)     Record the wages expense**

**(ii)    Record the HMRC liability**

**(iii)   Record the net wages paid to the employees**

**(iv)   Record the trade union liability.**

(i)

| Account name | Amount £ | Debit ✓ | Credit ✓ |
|---|---|---|---|
|  |  |  |  |
|  |  |  |  |

(ii)

| Account name | Amount £ | Debit ✓ | Credit ✓ |
|---|---|---|---|
|  |  |  |  |
|  |  |  |  |

(iii)

| Account name | Amount £ | Debit ✓ | Credit ✓ |
|---|---|---|---|
|  |  |  |  |
|  |  |  |  |

(iv)

| Account name | Amount £ | Debit ✓ | Credit ✓ |
|---|---|---|---|
|  |  |  |  |
|  |  |  |  |

Picklist for each: Bank, Employees NI, Employers NI, HMRC, Income tax, Net wages, Pension, Trade union, Wages control, Wages expense.

# IRRECOVERABLE DEBTS, CONTRAS AND TYPES OF ERROR

## 12    BEDROOM BITS 2

A credit customer, ABC Ltd, has ceased trading, owing Bedroom Bits £2,400 including VAT.

**Record the journal entries needed in the general ledger to write off the net amount and the VAT.**

| Account name | Amount £ | Debit ✓ | Credit ✓ |
|---|---|---|---|
|  |  |  |  |
|  |  |  |  |
|  |  |  |  |

Picklist: Irrecoverable debts, ABC Ltd, Bedroom Bits, Purchases, Purchases ledger control, Sales, Sales ledger control, VAT.

## 13    GARDEN GATES 2

A credit customer, A B Landscapes Ltd, has ceased trading, owing Garden Gates £2,600 plus VAT at 20%.

**Record the journal entries needed in the general ledger to write off the net amount and the VAT.**

| Account name | Amount £ | Debit ✓ | Credit ✓ |
|---|---|---|---|
|  |  |  |  |
|  |  |  |  |
|  |  |  |  |

Picklist: Irrecoverable debts, A B Landscapes Ltd, Garden Gates, Purchases, Purchases ledger control, Sales, Sales ledger control, VAT.

### 14 CHESTNUT

On 1 December Chestnut had a balance of £46,000 on its Sales Ledger Control Account and £31,000 on its Purchase Ledger Control Account. It sold goods to Cook, one of its main suppliers, and was owed £4,000 by Cook at 1 December. Cook was owed £12,000 for goods it had sold to Chestnut.

**Perform a contra and balance off the ledger accounts below. Dates are not required.**

**SLCA**

| Details | Amount £ | Details | Amount £ |
|---------|----------|---------|----------|
|  |  |  |  |
|  |  |  |  |
|  |  |  |  |
|  |  |  |  |

**PLCA**

| Details | Amount £ | Details | Amount £ |
|---------|----------|---------|----------|
|  |  |  |  |
|  |  |  |  |
|  |  |  |  |
|  |  |  |  |

### 15 ALLEN

On 1 December Allen had a balance of £49,000 on its PLCA and £56,000 on its SLCA. It purchased goods from Dulieu, one of its main customers, and owed Dulieu £11,000 at 1 December. Dulieu owed Allen £23,000 for goods it had purchased from Allen.

**Perform a contra and balance off the ledger accounts below. Dates are not required.**

**SLCA**

| Details | Amount £ | Details | Amount £ |
|---------|----------|---------|----------|
|  |  |  |  |
|  |  |  |  |
|  |  |  |  |
|  |  |  |  |

**PLCA**

| Details | Amount £ | Details | Amount £ |
|---|---|---|---|
|  |  |  |  |
|  |  |  |  |
|  |  |  |  |
|  |  |  |  |

## 16    BEANZ

This is a customer's account in the sales ledger.

**Beanz Co**

| Details | Amount £ | Details | Amount £ |
|---|---|---|---|
| Balance b/f | 4,530 | Payment received | 2,100 |
| Invoice SD4564 | 3,210 | Credit note | 420 |

The customer has now ceased trading.

**Record the journal entries needed to write off the receivable in the general ledger including VAT.**

| Account name | Amount £ | Debit ✓ | Credit ✓ |
|---|---|---|---|
|  |  |  |  |
|  |  |  |  |
|  |  |  |  |

Picklist: Irrecoverable debts, Beanz Co, Purchases, Purchases ledger control, Sales, Sales ledger control, VAT.

## 17   ERROR TYPES 1

**Show which of the errors below are, or are not, disclosed by the trial balance.**

| Error in the general ledger | Error disclosed by the trial balance ✓ | Error NOT disclosed by the trial balance ✓ |
|---|---|---|
| Incorrectly calculating the balance on the Motor Vehicles account. | | |
| Recording a receipt for commission received in the bank interest received account. | | |
| Recording a bank receipt for bank interest received on the debit side of both the bank account and the bank interest received account. | | |
| Recording supplier invoices on the debit side of the purchase ledger control account and the credit side of the purchases account | | |
| Recording a payment by cheque to a payable in the purchase ledger control account only. | | |
| Recording a bank payment of £124 for insurance as £142 in the insurance account and £124 in the bank account. | | |

## 18   ERROR TYPES 2

**Show which of the errors below would cause an imbalance in the trial balance.**

| Error in the general ledger | Would cause imbalance ✓ | Would NOT cause imbalance ✓ |
|---|---|---|
| Recording a bank receipt for rent received on the credit side of both the bank account and rent received account. | | |
| Recording a payment for new machinery in the equipment hire account. | | |
| Recording a purchase return on the credit side of the purchase ledger control account and the debit side of the purchase returns account. | | |
| Incorrectly calculating the balance on the bank interest received account. | | |
| Recording a payment by cheque to a payable in the bank account only. | | |
| Recording a bank payment of £120 for stationery as £210 in both accounts. | | |

19    **ERROR TYPES 3**

Match each error description with the correct type of error by placing the appropriate answer in the table below.

| Error in the general ledger | Type of error |
|---|---|
| Recording a bank receipt for rent received on the credit side of both the bank account and rent received account. | |
| Recording a payment for new machinery in the equipment hire account. | |
| Recording a purchase return on the credit side of the PLCA and the debit side of the purchase returns account. | |

Picklist:  Transposition error, compensating error, error of original entry, error of omission, error of commission, error of principle, reversal of entries, casting error, single entry, extraction error, two entries on one side

20    **ERROR TYPES 4**

Match each error description with the correct type of error by placing the appropriate answer in the table below.

| Error in the general ledger | Type of error |
|---|---|
| Recording a payment to a payable in the bank account only. | |
| Recording a bank payment of £100 for stationery as £210 in both accounts. | |
| Recording a receipt for commission received in the bank interest received account. | |

Picklist for all above:  Transposition error, compensating error, error of original entry, error of omission, error of commission, error of principle, reversal of entries, casting error, single entry, extraction error, two entries on one side

21    **ERROR TYPES 5**

Match each error description with the correct type of error by placing the appropriate answer in the table below.

| Error in the general ledger | Type of error |
|---|---|
| A credit sale made at the month end was not recorded. | |
| Recording a bank payment of £120 for stationery as £210 in the stationery account and correctly in the bank account. | |
| Recording a receipt for commission received in the PLCA. | |

Picklist for all above:  Transposition error, compensating error, error of original entry, error of omission, error of commission, error of principle, reversal of entries, casting error, single entry, extraction error, two entries on one side.

## 22 ERROR TYPES 6

**Show which of the errors below would cause an imbalance in the trial balance.**

| Error in the general ledger | Would cause imbalance ✓ |
|---|---|
| Forgetting to post a journal to record a contra. | |
| Posting the VAT on a sale transaction as a debit rather than a credit. | |
| Recording a cash purchase in purchases and VAT only. | |
| Recording the electricity expense as a debit to wages expenses, with the corresponding entry correctly credited to cash. | |

## 23 PRINCIPLES

(a) **Show which error is an error of principle.**

| Error in the general ledger | ✓ |
|---|---|
| Incorrectly totalling up the sales day book. | |
| Recording a bank payment for rent on the debit side of the office equipment account. | |
| Recording rent received as a debit entry in the rent and rates account. | |
| Recording a payment to a supplier in the purchase ledger only. | |

(b) **Show which error represents two entries on one side.**

| Error in the general ledger | ✓ |
|---|---|
| Incorrectly totalling up the sales day book. | |
| Recording a bank payment for rent on the debit side of the office equipment account. | |
| Recording rent received as a debit entry in the rent and rates account. | |
| Recording a payment to a supplier in the purchase ledger only. | |

**24    EXTRACTION**

(a)    **Show which error is an error of extraction.**

| Error in the general ledger | ✓ |
|---|---|
| Incorrectly totalling up the sales day book. | |
| Totalling the sales day book correctly but entering the total into the SLCA as a credit balance. | |
| Recording drawings as a debit to drawings and a credit to cash. | |
| Forgetting to post the entries for payroll. | |

(b)    **Show which error represents an error of original entry.**

| Error in the general ledger | ✓ |
|---|---|
| Posting a £210 invoice for electricity as £210 in the electricity account but £120 in the bank account. | |
| Posting an invoice for electricity as a debit in both the electricity and bank accounts. | |
| Posting electricity expense as a credit to electricity and a debit to the bank account. | |
| Posting a £200 invoice for electricity as £210 in both the electricity and bank account. | |

# ERRORS

## 25 BANK ERROR

An entry to record a bank payment of £750 for repairs has been reversed.

**Record the journal entries needed in the general ledger to**

**(i)** remove the incorrect entry

**(ii)** record the correct entry.

(i)

| Account name | Amount £ | Debit ✓ | Credit ✓ |
|---|---|---|---|
| | | | |
| | | | |

(ii)

| Account name | Amount £ | Debit ✓ | Credit ✓ |
|---|---|---|---|
| | | | |
| | | | |

Picklist for all above: Bank, Cash, Rent, Purchases, Purchases ledger control, Repairs, Sales, Sales ledger control, Suspense, VAT.

## 26 RENT ERROR

An entry to record a bank receipt of £500 for rent received has been reversed.

**Record the journal entries needed in the general ledger to:**

**(i)** remove the incorrect entry

**(ii)** record the correct entry.

(i)

| Account name | Amount £ | Debit ✓ | Credit ✓ |
|---|---|---|---|
| | | | |
| | | | |

(ii)

| Account name | Amount £ | Debit ✓ | Credit ✓ |
|---|---|---|---|
| | | | |
| | | | |

Picklist for all above: Bank, Cash, Rent Received, Purchases, Purchases ledger control, Sales, Sales ledger control, Suspense, VAT.

## 27 GAS ERROR

An entry to record a gas expense of £300 was made correctly in the bank but was posted to electricity expenses instead of gas expenses.

**Record the journal entries needed in the general ledger to record the correction.**

| Account name | Amount £ | Debit ✓ | Credit ✓ |
|---|---|---|---|
|  |  |  |  |
|  |  |  |  |

## 28 BUILDING ERROR

An entity purchased a new building for £400,000. This amount was debited to the buildings account, but £40,000 was credited to the bank account, requiring the creation of a suspense account.

**Record the journal entries needed in the general ledger to record the correction.**

| Account name | Amount £ | Debit ✓ | Credit ✓ |
|---|---|---|---|
|  |  |  |  |
|  |  |  |  |

## 29 SALES ERROR

A credit sale of £12,000 including VAT at 20% has been made. The full £12,000 has been debited to the SLCA and credited to sales.

**Record the journal entries needed in the general ledger to record the correction.**

| Account name | Amount £ | Debit ✓ | Credit ✓ |
|---|---|---|---|
|  |  |  |  |
|  |  |  |  |

## 30 MOTOR ERROR

An entity incurred costs of £700 to repair a motor vehicle, which it has debited to the motor vehicles account.

**Record the journal entries needed in the general ledger to record the correction.**

| Account name | Amount £ | Debit ✓ | Credit ✓ |
|---|---|---|---|
|  |  |  |  |
|  |  |  |  |

## 31 INVENTORY ERROR

An entity purchased goods for £720 including VAT at 20%, but recorded the purchase as £270 including VAT in the purchase day book.

**Record the journal entries needed in the general ledger to record the correction.**

| Account name | Amount £ | Debit ✓ | Credit ✓ |
|---|---|---|---|
|  |  |  |  |
|  |  |  |  |
|  |  |  |  |

## 32 PLANT ERROR

A junior member of the accounts team has processed the plant depreciation journal by debiting £12,000 to the plant accumulated depreciation account and crediting £12,000 to the depreciation expense account.

**Record the journal entries needed in the general ledger to record the correction.**

| Account name | Amount £ | Debit ✓ | Credit ✓ |
|---|---|---|---|
|  |  |  |  |
|  |  |  |  |

## 33 PURCHASE ERROR

A credit purchase of £9,000 including VAT at 20% has been made. The full £9,000 has been debited to purchases and credited to the purchase ledger control account.

**Record the journal entries needed in the general ledger to record the correction.**

| Account name | Amount £ | Debit ✓ | Credit ✓ |
|---|---|---|---|
|  |  |  |  |
|  |  |  |  |

## 34 INSURANCE ERROR

A payment for insurance of £2,700 has been made. The correct amount has been debited to the insurance expense account and credited to the purchase ledger control account.

**Record the journal entries needed in the general ledger to record the correction.**

| Account name | Amount £ | Debit ✓ | Credit ✓ |
|---|---|---|---|
|  |  |  |  |
|  |  |  |  |

# BALANCING THE TRIAL BALANCE AND CORRECTION OF ERRORS

**35   CB INTERIORS**

CB Interiors' initial trial balance includes a suspense account with a balance of £8,640.

The error has been traced to the purchase day-book shown below.

Purchase day-book

| Date | Details | Invoice number | Total £ | VAT £ | Net £ |
|---|---|---|---|---|---|
| 30 Jun | Able Paints Ltd | 2763 | 2,400 | 400 | 2,000 |
| 30 Jun | Matley Materials | 2764 | 3,120 | 520 | 2,600 |
| 30 Jun | Teesdale Parts | 2765 | 4,080 | 680 | 3,400 |
|  |  |  |  |  |  |
|  |  |  |  |  |  |
|  | **Totals** |  | 960 | 1,600 | 8,000 |

**Identify the error and record the journal entries needed in the general ledger to**

**(i)      remove the incorrect entry**

**(ii)     record the correct entry**

**(iii)    remove the suspense account balance.**

(i)

| Account name | Amount £ | Debit ✓ | Credit ✓ |
|---|---|---|---|
|  |  |  |  |

(ii)

| Account name | Amount £ | Debit ✓ | Credit ✓ |
|---|---|---|---|
|  |  |  |  |

(iii)

| Account name | Amount £ | Debit ✓ | Credit ✓ |
|---|---|---|---|
|  |  |  |  |

Picklist for all above: Able Paints Ltd, Matley Materials, Teesdale Parts, Purchases, Purchases day-book, Purchases ledger control, Purchases returns, Purchases returns day-book, Sales, Sales day-book, Sales ledger control, Sales returns, Sales returns day-book, Suspense, VAT.

## 36  ROGER DODGER

Roger Dodger's initial trial balance includes a suspense account with a balance of £360.

The error has been traced to the purchase returns day-book shown below.

Purchase returns day-book

| DATE 20XX | Details | Note number | Total £ | VAT £ | Net £ |
|---|---|---|---|---|---|
| 30 Jun | Dennis Designs Ltd | 421 | 1,200 | 200 | 1,000 |
| 30 Jun | XYZ Ltd | 422 | 1,920 | 320 | 1,600 |
| 30 Jun | Denby Prints | 423 | 4,800 | 800 | 4,000 |
| | | | | | |
| | | | | | |
| | Totals | | 7,920 | 1,680 | 6,600 |

**Identify the error and record the journal entries needed in the general ledger to:**

**(i)** **remove the incorrect entry**

**(ii)** **record the correct entry**

**(iii)** **remove the suspense account balance.**

(i)

| Account name | Amount £ | Debit ✔ | Credit ✔ |
|---|---|---|---|
| | | | |

(ii)

| Account name | Amount £ | Debit ✔ | Credit ✔ |
|---|---|---|---|
| | | | |

(iii)

| Account name | Amount £ | Debit ✔ | Credit ✔ |
|---|---|---|---|
| | | | |

Picklist for all above: Dennis Designs Ltd, XYZ Ltd, Denby Prints, Purchases, Purchases day-book, Purchases ledger control, Purchases returns, Purchases returns day-book,  Sales, Sales day-book, Sales ledger control, Sales returns, Sales returns day-book, Suspense, VAT.

**37 A CUT ABOVE**

A Cut Above's initial trial balance includes a suspense account with a balance of £230.

The error has been traced to the purchase returns day-book shown below.

**Purchases returns day-book**

| Date 20XX | Details | Returns note number | Total £ | VAT £ | Net £ |
|---|---|---|---|---|---|
| 30 April | A & S Timber Ltd | 12 – 356K | 576 | 96 | 480 |
| 30 April | GB Tools | AB768 – 2 | 816 | 136 | 680 |
| 30 April | LAH Ltd | 236 | 4,560 | 760 | 3,800 |
| | | | | | |
| | | | | | |
| | Totals | | 6,182 | 992 | 4,960 |

**Identify the error and record the journal entries needed in the general ledger to:**

**(i)   remove the incorrect entry**

**(ii)   record the correct entry**

**(iii)   remove the suspense account balance.**

(i)

| Account name | Amount £ | Debit ✔ | Credit ✔ |
|---|---|---|---|
| | | | |

(ii)

| Account name | Amount £ | Debit ✔ | Credit ✔ |
|---|---|---|---|
| | | | |

(iii)

| Account name | Amount £ | Debit ✔ | Credit ✔ |
|---|---|---|---|
| | | | |

Picklist for all above: A & S Timber Ltd, GB Tools, LAH Ltd, Purchases, Purchases day-book, Purchases ledger control, Purchases returns, Purchase returns day-books, Sales, Sales day-book, Sales ledger control, Sales returns, Sales returns day-books, Suspense, VAT.

## 38   RESTCO

Restco's initial trial balance includes a suspense account with a balance of £720.

The error has been traced to the sales day-book shown below.

Sales day-book

| Date 20XX | Details | Invoice number | Total £ | VAT £ | Net £ |
|---|---|---|---|---|---|
| 30 Jun | Ben's Build Ltd | 11232 | 2,160 | 360 | 1,800 |
| 30 Jun | OPP Ltd | 11233 | 3,360 | 560 | 2,800 |
| 30 Jun | Outside Capers | 11234 | 5,040 | 840 | 4,200 |
| | | | | | |
| | | | | | |
| | Totals | | 10,560 | 1,760 | 8,080 |

**Identify the error and record the journal entries needed in the general ledger to**

**(i)    remove the incorrect entry**

**(ii)    record the correct entry**

**(iii)    remove the suspense account balance.**

(i)

| Account name | Amount £ | Debit ✓ | Credit ✓ |
|---|---|---|---|
| | | | |

(ii)

| Account name | Amount £ | Debit ✓ | Credit ✓ |
|---|---|---|---|
| | | | |

(iii)

| Account name | Amount £ | Debit ✓ | Credit ✓ |
|---|---|---|---|
| | | | |

Picklist for all above: Ben's Build Ltd, OPP Ltd, Outside Capers, Purchases, Purchases day-book, Purchases ledger control, Purchases returns, Purchases returns day-book, Sales, Sales day-book, Sales ledger control, Sales returns, Sales returns day-book, Suspense, VAT.

**39    JOHNNY JOINER**

Johnny Joiner's trial balance was extracted and did not balance.  The debit column of the trial balance totalled £442,735 and the credit column totalled £428,372.

**(a)    What entry would be made in the suspense account to balance the trial balance?**

| Account name | Amount £ | Debit ✓ | Credit ✓ |
|---|---|---|---|
| Suspense | | | |

**(b)**    The error has been traced to sales, which were posted as £241,874 instead of £256,237.

**Record the journal entries needed in the general ledger to record the correction.**

| Account name | Amount £ | Debit ✓ | Credit ✓ |
|---|---|---|---|
| | | | |
| | | | |

**40    BUCKLEY DRAINS**

Buckley Drains' trial balance was extracted and did not balance.  The debit column of the trial balance totalled £336,728 and the credit column totalled £325,923.

**(a)    What entry would be made in the suspense account to balance the trial balance?**

| Account name | Amount £ | Debit ✓ | Credit ✓ |
|---|---|---|---|
| Suspense | | | |

**(b)**    The error has been traced to an unpaid invoice for advertising, which was recorded correctly in advertising expenses but nowhere else.

**Record the journal entries needed in the general ledger to record the correction.**

| Account name | Amount £ | Debit ✓ | Credit ✓ |
|---|---|---|---|
| | | | |
| | | | |

**(c)    Show one reason for maintaining the journal**

| | ✓ |
|---|---|
| To correct errors only | |
| To correct errors and record transactions that have not been recorded in any other book of prime entry | |
| To record transactions from every other book of prime entry. | |

## 41   MENDONCA

Mendonca's trial balance was extracted and did not balance.  The debit column of the trial balance totalled £643,475 and the credit column totalled £641,495

**(a)**   **What entry would be made in the suspense account to balance the trial balance?**

| Account name | Amount £ | Debit ✓ | Credit ✓ |
|---|---|---|---|
|  |  |  |  |

**(b)**   The error has been traced to the posting of the wages payment. The total payment made was £3,200. This was incorrectly made in both the wages and bank account. The amount recorded in wages was £2,300, with a credit made to the bank of £320.

**Record the journal entries needed in the general ledger to record the correction.**

| Account name | Amount £ | Debit ✓ | Credit ✓ |
|---|---|---|---|
|  |  |  |  |
|  |  |  |  |
|  |  |  |  |

## 42   BEASANT

Beasant's trial balance was extracted and did not balance.  The debit column of the trial balance totalled £630,000 and the credit column totalled £615,000.

**(a)**   **What entry would be made in the suspense account to balance the trial balance?**

| Account name | Amount £ | Debit ✓ | Credit ✓ |
|---|---|---|---|
| Suspense |  |  |  |

**(b)**   The error has been traced to a late credit sale. The full amount of the sale (including VAT at 20%) was correctly recorded in the SLCA but no other entries were made.

**Record the journal entries needed in the general ledger to record the correction.**

| Account name | Amount £ | Debit ✓ | Credit ✓ |
|---|---|---|---|
|  |  |  |  |
|  |  |  |  |
|  |  |  |  |

**(c)**   **Show one reason for maintaining the journal**

|  | ✓ |
|---|---|
| To detect fraud |  |
| To record non-regular transactions |  |
| To record goods sold on credit |  |

# POSTING JOURNAL ENTRIES TO LEDGER ACCOUNTS

### 43    PAT'S CAFE

Pat's Cafe's trial balance did not balance. The debit column totalled £67,410 and the credit column totalled £72,060.

**(a)    What entry would be made in the suspense account to balance the trial balance?**

| Account name | Amount £ | Debit ✓ | Credit ✓ |
|---|---|---|---|
|  |  |  |  |

The journal entries to correct the bookkeeping errors, and a list of balances as they appear in the trial balance, are shown below.

**Journal entries**

| Account name | Debit £ | Credit £ |
|---|---|---|
| Bank interest paid | 114 |  |
| Bank interest received |  | 114 |
|  |  |  |
| Insurance | 150 |  |
| Suspense |  | 150 |
|  |  |  |
| Motor vehicles | 4,500 |  |
| Suspense |  | 4,500 |

**Account name**

| Account name | Debit £ | Credit £ |
|---|---|---|
| Bank interest paid | 121 |  |
| Bank interest received | 53 |  |
| Insurance | 400 |  |
| Motor vehicles | 2000 |  |

**(b)    Complete the table below to show the new balances, and whether each will be a debit or a credit.**

| Account name | Balance £ | Debit ✓ | Credit ✓ |
|---|---|---|---|
| Bank interest paid |  |  |  |
| Bank interest received |  |  |  |
| Insurance |  |  |  |
| Motor vehicles |  |  |  |

## 44 TWINKLE'S TRINKETS

Twinkle's Trinkets trial balance did not balance. The debit column totalled £112,340 and the credit column totalled £111,564.

**(a)** **What entry would be made in the suspense account to balance the trial balance?**

| Account name | Amount £ | Debit ✓ | Credit ✓ |
|---|---|---|---|
| Suspense | | | |

The journal entries to correct the bookkeeping errors, and a list of balances as they appear in the trial balance, are shown below.

**Journal entries**

| Account name | Debit £ | Credit £ |
|---|---|---|
| Motor expenses | 324 | |
| Suspense | | 324 |
| | | |
| Suspense | 1,100 | |
| Repairs and renewals | | 1,100 |
| | | |
| Rent payable | 500 | |
| Rent received | | 500 |

**Account name**

| Account name | Debit £ | Credit £ |
|---|---|---|
| Motor expenses | 8,420 | |
| Repairs and renewals | 2,310 | |
| Rent payable | 3,200 | |
| Rent received | | 1,200 |

**(b)** **Complete the table below to show the new balances, and whether each will be a debit or a credit.**

| Account name | Balance £ | Debit ✓ | Credit ✓ |
|---|---|---|---|
| Motor expenses | | | |
| Repairs and renewals | | | |
| Rent payable | | | |
| Rent received | | | |

## 45    SPARKS AND MENCER

Sparks and Mencer's trial balance included a suspense account.  All the bookkeeping errors have now been traced and the journal entries shown below have been recorded.

The journal entries to correct the bookkeeping errors, and a list of balances as they appear in the trial balance, are shown below.

**Journal entries**

| Account name | Debit £ | Credit £ |
|---|---|---|
| Heat and light | | 545 |
| Suspense | 545 | |
| | | |
| Rates | 786 | |
| Suspense | | 786 |
| | | |
| Loan interest expense | 269 | |
| Rent received | | 269 |

**Account name**

| Account name | Debit £ | Credit £ |
|---|---|---|
| Heat and light | 1,200 | |
| Rates | 630 | |
| Loan interest expense | | 104 |
| Rent received | 150 | |

**Complete the table below to show the new balances, and whether each will be a debit or a credit.**

| Account name | Balance £ | Debit ✓ | Credit ✓ |
|---|---|---|---|
| Heat and light | | | |
| Rates | | | |
| Loan interest expense | | | |
| Rent received | | | |

# RE-DRAFT THE TRIAL BALANCE

### 46   RICK'S RACERS

On 30 June Rick's Racers extracted an initial trial balance which did not balance, and a suspense account was opened.  On 1 July journal entries were prepared to correct the errors that had been found, and clear the suspense account.  The list of balances in the initial trial balance, and the journal entries to correct the errors, are shown below.

**Re-draft the trial balance by placing the figures in the debit or credit column.  You should take into account the journal entries which will clear the suspense account.**

| | Original balances extracted on 30 June £ | New balance following adjustment on 1 July £ | Debit ✓ | Credit ✓ |
|---|---|---|---|---|
| Motor vehicles | 24,200 | | | |
| Plant and equipment | 22,350 | | | |
| Inventory | 9,000 | | | |
| Cash at bank | 11,217 | | | |
| Cash | 150 | | | |
| Sales ledger control | 131,275 | | | |
| Purchases ledger control | 75,336 | | | |
| VAT owing to HMRC | 15,127 | | | |
| Capital | 14,417 | | | |
| Bank loan | 12,500 | | | |
| Sales | 276,132 | | | |
| Purchases | 152,476 | | | |
| Wages | 35,465 | | | |
| Motor expenses | 3,617 | | | |
| Repairs and renewals | 2,103 | | | |
| Rent and rates | 3,283 | | | |
| Light and heat | 4,012 | | | |
| Insurance | 4,874 | | | |
| Sundry expenses | 1,230 | | | |
| Suspense account (credit balance) | 11,740 | | | |

**Journal entries**

| Account name | Debit £ | Credit £ |
|---|---|---|
| Capital | | 9,500 |
| Suspense | 9,500 | |
| Capital | | 2,330 |
| Suspense | 2,330 | |

| Account name | Debit £ | Credit £ |
|---|---|---|
| Suspense | 1,230 | |
| Sundry expenses | | 1,230 |
| Sundry expenses | 1,320 | |
| Suspense | | 1,320 |

## 47 PERCY POTS

On 30 June Percy Pots extracted an initial trial balance which did not balance, and a suspense account was opened.  On 1 July journal entries were prepared to correct the errors that had been found, and clear the suspense account.  The list of balances in the initial trial balance, and the journal entries to correct the errors, are shown below.

**Re-draft the trial balance by placing the figures in the debit or credit column.  You should take into account the journal entries which will clear the suspense account.**

| | Balances extracted on 30 June £ | Balances at 1 July | |
|---|---|---|---|
| | | Debit £ | Credit £ |
| Motor vehicles | 22,348 | | |
| Fixtures and fittings | 9,234 | | |
| Inventory | 4,800 | | |
| Bank | 2,661 | | |
| Petty cash | 100 | | |
| Sales ledger control | 61,025 | | |
| Purchases ledger control | 35,275 | | |
| VAT owing to HMRC | 4,630 | | |
| Capital | 4,852 | | |
| Sales | 142,378 | | |
| Sales returns | 1,780 | | |
| Purchases | 69,276 | | |
| Wages | 13,500 | | |
| Motor expenses | 873 | | |
| Office expenses | 1,796 | | |
| Rent and rates | 1,276 | | |
| Heat and light | 1,022 | | |
| Insurance | 1,629 | | |
| Miscellaneous expenses | 1,047 | | |
| Suspense account (credit balance) | 5,232 | | |
| **Totals** | | | |

**Journal entries**

| Account name | Debit £ | Credit £ |
|---|---|---|
| Bank | | 2,661 |
| Suspense | 2,661 | |
| Bank | | 2,661 |
| Suspense | 2,661 | |

| Account name | Debit £ | Credit £ |
|---|---|---|
| Sales returns | 1,870 | |
| Suspense | | 1,870 |
| Sales returns | | 1,780 |
| Suspense | 1,780 | |

## 48 IVOR ISLAND

On 30 April Ivor Island extracted an initial trial balance which did not balance, and a suspense account was opened. On 1 May journal entries were prepared to correct the errors that had been found, and clear the suspense account. The list of balances in the initial trial balance, and the journal entries to correct the errors, are shown below.

**Redraft the trial balance by placing the figures in the debit or credit column. You should take into account the journal entries below which will clear the suspense account.**

| | | Balances at 1 May | |
|---|---|---|---|
| | Balances extracted on 30 April | Debit £ | Credit £ |
| Motor vehicles | 8,454 | | |
| Office building | 28,676 | | |
| Inventory | 15,369 | | |
| Bank | 26,984 | | |
| Petty cash | 459 | | |
| Sales ledger control | 35,987 | | |
| Purchases ledger control | 26,942 | | |
| VAT (owing from HMRC) | 231 | | |
| Capital | 98,106 | | |
| Sales | 96,325 | | |
| Purchase returns (credit balance) | 3,654 | | |
| Purchases | 68,975 | | |
| Wages | 18,564 | | |
| Motor expenses | 1,269 | | |
| Office expenses | 5,798 | | |
| Rates | 4,300 | | |
| Heat and light | 5,423 | | |
| Insurance | 3,365 | | |
| Miscellaneous expenses | 2,645 | | |
| Suspense account (credit balance) | 1,472 | | |

**Journal entries:**

| Account name | Debit £ | Credit £ |
|---|---|---|
| VAT | | 586 |
| Suspense | 586 | |
| VAT | | 586 |
| Suspense | 586 | |

| Account name | Debit £ | Credit £ |
|---|---|---|
| Purchase returns | | 2,556 |
| Suspense | 2,556 | |
| Purchase returns | 2,256 | |
| Suspense | | 2,256 |

## 49 RING OF ROSES

On 30 June Ring of Roses extracted an initial trial balance which did not balance, and a suspense account was opened. On 1 July journal entries were prepared to correct the errors that had been found, and clear the suspense account. The list of balances in the initial trial balance, and the journal entries to correct the errors, are shown below.

**Re-draft the trial balance by placing the figures in the debit or credit column. You should take into account the journal entries which will clear the suspense account.**

| | Balances extracted on 30 June £ | Balances at 1 July Debit £ | Credit £ |
|---|---|---|---|
| Motor vehicles | 27,625 | | |
| Plant and equipment | 5,000 | | |
| Inventory | 7,350 | | |
| Cash at bank | 7,195 | | |
| Cash | 200 | | |
| Sales ledger control | 121,275 | | |
| Purchases ledger control | 67,323 | | |
| VAT owing to HMRC | 10,098 | | |
| Capital | 22,291 | | |
| Sales | 253,727 | | |
| Sales returns | 2,123 | | |
| Purchases | 128,476 | | |
| Purchase returns | 9,872 | | |
| Wages | 34,250 | | |
| Motor expenses | 1,797 | | |
| Office expenses | 4,946 | | |
| Rent and rates | 2,321 | | |
| Heat and light | 3,123 | | |
| Insurance | 4,205 | | |
| Suspense account (debit balance) | 13,425 | | |
| **Totals** | | | |

**Journal entries**

| Account name | Debit £ | Credit £ |
|---|---|---|
| Bank | 7,150 | |
| Suspense | | 7,150 |
| Purchases | 6,455 | |
| Suspense | | 6,455 |
| Suspense | 4,205 | |
| Insurance | | 4,205 |
| Insurance | 4,025 | |
| Suspense | | 4,025 |

## 50    HEARN

On 30 June Hearn extracted an initial trial balance which did not balance, and a suspense account was opened.  On 1 July the following errors were noted:

1    A rent payment of £430 had been correctly included in the bank, but included within rent expenses as £340.

2    An irrecoverable debt of £600 plus VAT at 20% had been credited correctly to the SLCA, but the only debit entry was £600 to irrecoverable debts.

**Complete the journal to correct the errors, and re-draft the trial balance by placing figures into the debit or credit column. Your re-drafted trial balance should take into account the journal entries you have made.**

**Journal entries**

| Account name | Debit £ | Credit £ |
|---|---|---|
| | | |
| | | |
| | | |
| | | |

| | Balances extracted on 30 June £ | Balances at 1 July | |
|---|---|---|---|
| | | Debit £ | Credit £ |
| Sales ledger control | 34,560 | | |
| Purchases ledger control | 21,420 | | |
| VAT owing to HMRC | 3,412 | | |
| Capital | 50,000 | | |
| Sales | 201,327 | | |
| Sales returns | 1,465 | | |
| Purchases | 87,521 | | |
| Purchase returns | 252 | | |
| Plant and equipment | 15,200 | | |
| Motor expenses | 4,310 | | |
| Office expenses | 10,321 | | |
| Rent and rates | 21,420 | | |
| Heat and light | 8,920 | | |
| Wages | 53,205 | | |
| Irrecoverable debt | 1,450 | | |
| Office equipment | 42,030 | | |
| Bank overdraft | 4201 | | |
| Suspense account (debit balance) | 210 | | |
| | **Totals** | | |

**51 RODMAN**

On 30 June Rodman extracted an initial trial balance which did not balance, and a suspense account was opened. On 1 July the following errors were noted:

1    A VAT refund of £1,250 received from HMRC was recorded in the bank, but no other entry was made.

2    A wages payment of £4,300 was credited to both the bank and wages.

**Complete the journal to correct the errors, and re-draft the trial balance by placing figures into the debit or credit column. Your re-drafted trial balance should take into account the journal entries you have made.**

**Journal entries**

| Account name | Debit £ | Credit £ |
|---|---|---|
| | | |
| | | |
| | | |
| | | |

| | Balances extracted on 30 June £ | Balances at 1 July Debit £ | Credit £ |
|---|---|---|---|
| Sales ledger control | 38,070 | | |
| Purchases ledger control | 20,310 | | |
| VAT owed from HMRC | 2,510 | | |
| Capital | 70,000 | | |
| Sales | 153,488 | | |
| Sales returns | 2,135 | | |
| Purchases | 63,261 | | |
| Purchase returns | 542 | | |
| Plant and equipment | 17,319 | | |
| Motor expenses | 3,214 | | |
| Office expenses | 6,421 | | |
| Rent and rates | 17,414 | | |
| Heat and light | 6,421 | | |
| Wages | 45,532 | | |
| Irrecoverable debt | 1,532 | | |
| Office equipment | 35,313 | | |
| Bank overdraft | 2,152 | | |
| Suspense account (debit balance) | 7,350 | | |
| **Totals** | | | |

# UPDATE THE CASH BOOK

### 52   RIVERS LTD

The bank statement and cash book of Rivers is shown below.

| **Midway Bank PLC** | | | | |
|---|---|---|---|---|
| **52 The Parade, Middleton, MD1 9LA** | | | | |
| To: Rivers Ltd | Account No: 28012877 | | 23 June 20XX | |
| **Statement of Account** | | | | |
| **Date 20XX** | **Detail** | **Paid out £** | **Paid in £** | **Balance £** |
| 04 June | Balance b/d | | | 3,115 C |
| 04 June | Cheque 101013 | 650 | | 2,465 C |
| 04 June | Cheque 101014 | 1,420 | | 1,045 C |
| 05 June | Cheque 101015 | 60 | | 985 C |
| 07 June | Cheque 101018 | 450 | | 535 C |
| 12 June | Bank Giro Credit Ayreshire Build | | 970 | 1,505 C |
| 13 June | Cheque 101016 | 615 | | 890 C |
| 15 June | Direct debit Collins | 175 | | 715 C |
| 19 June | Paid in at Midway bank | | 300 | 1,015 C |
| 20 June | Direct Debit rent | 500 | | 515 C |
| 23 June | Bank interest | | 15 | 530 C |
| 23 June | Bank charges | 20 | | 510 C |
| D = Debit   C = Credit | | | | |

| Date 20XX | Details | Bank £ | Date 20XX | Cheque number | Details | Bank £ |
|---|---|---|---|---|---|---|
| 01 June | Balance b/d | 3,115 | 01 June | 101013 | Indigo Beds | 650 |
| 17 June | Bracken Ltd | 300 | 01 June | 101014 | DirectFit | 1,420 |
| 21 June | Airfleet Interiors | 560 | 01 June | 101015 | Langdon | 60 |
| 22 June | Harris Homes | 333 | 02 June | 101016 | QPF Ltd | 615 |
| | | | 03 June | 101017 | OMD Ltd | 815 |
| | | | 03 June | 101018 | Hamden Ltd | 450 |
| | | | 15 June | 101019 | Freeman and Cope | 522 |
| | | | 15 June | | Collins | 175 |
| | | | | | | |
| | | | | | | |
| | | | | | | |
| | | | | | | |
| | | | | | | |

Details columns options: Balance b/d, Balance c/d, Bank charges, QPF Ltd, Bracken Ltd, Ayreshire Build, Closing balance, Directfit, Hamden Ltd, Rent, Collins, Langdon, Airfleet Interiors, Freeman and Cope, OMD Ltd, Opening balance, Bank Interest, Indigo Beds, Harris Homes.

(a)    Check the items on the bank statement against the items in the cash book.

(b)    Enter any items in the cash book as needed.

(c)    Total the cash book and clearly show the balance carried down at 23 June (closing balance) and brought down at 24 June (opening balance).

## 53    LUXURY BATHROOMS

On 28 April Luxury Bathrooms received the following bank statement as at 24 April.

| | **SKB Bank plc** | | | | |
|---|---|---|---|---|---|
| | **68 London Road, Reading, RG8 4RN** | | | | |
| To: Luxury Bathrooms | Account No: 55548921 | | | 24 April 20XX | |
| | **Statement of Account** | | | | |
| **Date** | **Detail** | **Paid out** | **Paid in** | **Balance** | |
| **20XX** | | £ | £ | £ | |
| 03 April | Balance b/d | | | 17,845 | C |
| 03 April | Cheque 120045 | 8,850 | | 8,995 | C |
| 04 April | Bank Giro Credit Ricketts & Co | | 465 | 9,460 | C |
| 04 April | Cheque 120046 | 2,250 | | 7,210 | C |
| 05 April | Cheque 120047 | 64 | | 7,146 | C |
| 08 April | Cheque 120048 | 3,256 | | 3,890 | C |
| 14 April | Direct Debit AMB Ltd | 2,265 | | 1,625 | C |
| 14 April | Direct Debit D Draper | 2,950 | | 1,325 | D |
| 14 April | Cheque 120050 | 655 | | 1,980 | D |
| 22 April | Paid in at SKB bank | | 2,150 | 170 | C |
| 22 April | Bank charges | 63 | | 107 | C |
| 23 April | Overdraft fee | 25 | | 82 | C |
| | D = Debit   C = Credit | | | | |

The cash book as at 24 April is shown below.

**Cash book**

| Date | Details | Bank | Date | Cheque | Details | Bank |
|---|---|---|---|---|---|---|
| 01 April | Balance b/d | 17,845 | 01 April | 120045 | R Sterling Ltd | 8,850 |
| 19 April | Olsen & Lane | 2,150 | 01 April | 120046 | Bert Cooper | 2,250 |
| 22 April | Frith Ltd | 685 | 01 April | 120047 | Hetko & Sons | 64 |
| 22 April | Hodgetts & Co | 282 | 02 April | 120048 | Barrett Ltd | 3,256 |
| | | | 02 April | 120049 | K Plomer | 542 |
| | | | 08 April | 120050 | I&E Brown | 655 |
| | | | 08 April | 120051 | T Roberts | 1,698 |
| | | | 14 April | | AMB Ltd | 2,265 |
| | | | | | | |
| | | | | | | |
| | | | | | | |
| | | | | | | |
| | | | | | | |
| | | | | | | |

Details column options: Balance b/d, balance c/d, Bank charges, R Sterling Ltd, Olsen & Lane, Frith Ltd, Hodgetts & Co, Bert Cooper, Hetko & Sons, Barrett Ltd, K Plomer, I&E Brown, T Roberts, AMB Ltd, Ricketts & Co, D Draper, Opening balance, Overdraft fees.

(a) Check the items on the bank statement against the items in the cash book.

(b) Enter any items in the cash book as needed.

(c) Total the cash book and clearly show the balance carried down at 24 April (closing balance) and brought down at 25 April (opening balance).

## 54 WHOLESALE FLOORING

The bank statement and cash book for Wholesale Flooring is shown below.

**Money Bags Bank PLC**
**52 Oak Road, Timperley, SK10 8LR**

To: Wholesale Flooring          Account No: 47013799          23 June 20XX

**Statement of Account**

| Date 20XX | Detail | Paid out £ | Paid in £ | Balance £ | |
|---|---|---|---|---|---|
| 04 June | Balance b/d | | | 5,125 | D |
| 05 June | Cheque 104373 | 890 | | 6,015 | D |
| 05 June | Cheque 104374 | 1,725 | | 7,740 | D |
| 05 June | Cheque 104375 | 210 | | 7,950 | D |
| 11 June | Cheque 104378 | 784 | | 8,734 | D |
| 12 June | Bank Giro Credit Aintree and Co | | 1,250 | 7,484 | D |
| 13 June | Cheque 104376 | 1,275 | | 8,759 | D |
| 15 June | Cheque 104377 | 725 | | 9,484 | D |
| 17 June | Paid in at Money Bags Bank plc | | 550 | 8,934 | D |
| 20 June | Direct debit MD County Council | 400 | | 9,334 | D |
| 23 June | Bank charges | 160 | | 9,494 | D |
| 23 June | Overdraft fee | 90 | | 9,584 | D |
| | D = Debit   C = Credit | | | | |

**Cash book**

| Date 20XX | Details | Bank £ | Date 20XX | Cheque number | Details | Bank £ |
|---|---|---|---|---|---|---|
| | | | 01 June | | Balance b/d | 5,125 |
| 16 June | Beeston's | 550 | 01 June | 104373 | Good Iron | 890 |
| 19 June | Airfleet Exteriors | 3,025 | 01 June | 104374 | Ashworth & Co | 1,725 |
| 22 June | Jones's | 2,775 | 01 June | 104375 | Ironfit | 210 |
| | | | 05 June | 104376 | OSS Ltd | 1,275 |
| | | | 07 June | 104377 | Perfect Tools | 725 |
| | | | 08 June | 104378 | Campden Ltd | 784 |
| | | | 14 June | 104379 | Thornley & Thwaite | 675 |
| | | | 14 June | 104380 | Castle & Cove | 178 |
| | | | | | | |
| | | | | | | |
| | | | | | | |
| | | | | | | |
| | | | | | | |

Details columns options: Balance b/d, Balance c/d, Bank charges, Good Iron, Beeston's, Aintree & Co, Perfect Tools, Closing balance, Ashworth & Co, Thornley & Thwaite, MD County Council, Campden Ltd, Airfleet Exteriors, Castle & Cove, OSS Ltd, Opening balance, Overdraft Fee, Ironfit, Jones's.

(a) **Check the items on the bank statement against the items in the cash book.**

(b) **Enter any items in the cash book as needed.**

(c) **Total the cash book and clearly show the balance carried down at 23 June (closing balance) and brought down at 24 June (opening balance).**

## 55 24 HOUR TAXIS

On 28 June 24 Hour Taxis received the following bank statement as at 23 June.

| | Four Kings Bank PLC | | | |
|---|---|---|---|---|
| | **124 Four Kings Way, Newton Mearns, GL10 5QR** | | | |
| To: 24 Hour Taxis | Account No: 16135844 | | 23 June 20XX | |

**Statement of Account**

| Date 20XX | Detail | Paid out £ | Paid in £ | Balance £ | |
|---|---|---|---|---|---|
| 04 June | Balance b/d | | | 6,025 | C |
| 05 June | Cheque 102597 | 910 | | 5,115 | C |
| 05 June | Cheque 102598 | 2,010 | | 3,105 | C |
| 05 June | Cheque 102599 | 315 | | 2,790 | C |
| 11 June | Cheque 102602 | 675 | | 2,115 | C |
| 12 June | Bank Giro Credit Barron Homes | | 1,475 | 3,590 | C |
| 13 June | Cheque 102600 | 1,725 | | 1,865 | C |
| 15 June | Cheque 102601 | 686 | | 1,179 | C |
| 17 June | Paid in at Four Kings Bank | | 1,000 | 2,179 | C |
| 20 June | Direct Debit AB Insurance | 1,250 | | 929 | C |
| 23 June | Bank charges | 50 | | 879 | C |
| 23 June | Overdraft fee | 25 | | 854 | C |
| | D = Debit   C = Credit | | | | |

**Cash book**

| Date 20XX | Details | Bank £ | Date 20XX | Cheque number | Details | Bank £ |
|---|---|---|---|---|---|---|
| 01 June | Balance b/d | 6,025 | 01 June | 102597 | Best Ideas | 910 |
| 18 June | Earnshaw's | 1,000 | 02 June | 102598 | Bentley & Burn | 2,010 |
| 19 June | Mainstreet Ltd | 1,206 | 02 June | 102599 | Bits & Bats | 315 |
| 21 June | Housley Inc | 1,725 | 03 June | 102600 | LPF Ltd | 1,725 |
| | | | 07 June | 102601 | Essentials | 686 |
| | | | 08 June | 102602 | Hopburn Ltd | 675 |
| | | | 15 June | 102603 | Thistle Tools | 410 |
| | | | 15 June | 102604 | C Campbell Ltd | 275 |
| | | | | | | |
| | | | | | | |
| | | | | | | |
| | | | | | | |

Details columns options: Balance b/d, Balance c/d, Bank charges, Earnshaw's, Housley Inc, C Campbell Ltd, Mainstreet Ltd, Closing balance, Barron Homes, Thistle Tools, AB Insurance, Hopburn Ltd, Best Ideas, Bentley & Burn, LPF Ltd, Opening balance, Overdraft Fee, Bits & Bats, Essentials.

(a)   Check the items on the bank statement against the items in the cash book.

(b)   Enter any items in the cash book as needed.

(c)   Total the cash book and clearly show the balance carried down at 23 June (closing balance) and brought down at 24 June (opening balance).

**56   WOOD**

The bank statement and cash book for Wood is shown below.

| | **Money Bags Bank PLC** | | | |
|---|---|---|---|---|
| | **52 Oak Road, Timperley, SK10 8LR** | | | |
| To: Wood Ltd | Account No: 47013799 | | 23 June 20XX | |

**Statement of Account**

| Date 20XX | Detail | Paid out £ | Paid in £ | Balance £ | |
|---|---|---|---|---|---|
| 04 June | Balance b/d | | | 17,640 | C |
| 05 June | Bank Giro Credit Bradley | | 1,320 | 18,960 | C |
| 05 June | Bank Giro Credit Thanoj | | 2,450 | 21,410 | C |
| 05 June | Paid in at Money Bags Bank PLC | | 9,420 | 30,830 | C |
| 11 June | Cheque 110341 | 1,540 | | 29,290 | C |
| 12 June | BACS payment Southwell | 820 | | 28,470 | C |
| 13 June | Cheque 110343 | 750 | | 27,720 | C |
| 15 June | Cheque 110344 | 570 | | 27,150 | C |
| 17 June | Interest earned | | 80 | 27,230 | C |
| 20 June | Direct debit Blundell | 400 | | 26,830 | C |
| 23 June | BACS payment Bore | 250 | | 26,580 | C |
| 23 June | Cheque 110346 | 740 | | 25,840 | C |

D = Debit   C = Credit

**Cash book**

| Date 20XX | Details | Bank £ | Date 20XX | Cheque number | Details | Bank £ |
|---|---|---|---|---|---|---|
| 01 June | Balance b/d | 17,640 | | | | |
| 03 June | Bradley | 1,320 | 04 June | 110341 | Carr | 1,540 |
| 03 June | Cash sales | 9,420 | 04 June | 110342 | Ramsden | 980 |
| 03 June | Thanoj | 2,450 | 04 June | 110343 | Coulson | 750 |
| 21 June | Cash sales | 7,430 | 04 June | 110344 | Brodie | 570 |
| 21 June | Devitt | 1,990 | 04 June | 110345 | Jones | 550 |
| | | | 04 June | 110346 | Gritton | 740 |
| | | | 20 June | | Bore | 250 |
| | | | | | | |
| | | | | | | |
| | | | | | | |
| | | | | | | |
| | | | | | | |

(a)  Check the items on the bank statement against the items in the cash book.

(b)  Enter any items in the cash book as needed.

(c)  Total the cash book and clearly show the balance carried down at 23 June (closing balance) and brought down at 24 June (opening balance).

## 57   PEARSON

The bank statement and cash book for Pearson is shown below:

| Money Bags Bank PLC | | | | | |
|---|---|---|---|---|---|
| To: Pearson Ltd | | Account No: 47013799 | | 23 June 20XX | |
| | | **Statement of Account** | | | |
| Date 20XX | Detail | Paid out £ | Paid in £ | Balance £ | |
| 01 June | Balance b/d | | | 1,340 | D |
| 02 June | Bank Giro Credit Pond | | 1,890 | 550 | C |
| 02 June | Interest received | | 5 | 555 | C |
| 02 June | Direct Debit McMenemy | 1,200 | | 645 | D |
| 11 June | Cheque 110123 | 430 | | 1,075 | D |
| 12 June | Paid in to Money Bags Bank | | 840 | 235 | D |
| 13 June | Cheque 110126 | 75 | | 310 | D |
| 15 June | Cheque 110127 | 270 | | 580 | D |
| 17 June | Paid in to Money Bags Bank | | 1,540 | 960 | C |
| 20 June | Direct debit Findus | 300 | | 660 | C |
| 23 June | Bank charges | 25 | | 635 | C |
| 23 June | Cheque 110129 | 740 | | 105 | D |
| D = Debit   C = Credit | | | | | |

**Cash book**

| Date 20XX | Details | Bank £ | Date 20XX | Cheque number | Details | Bank £ |
|---|---|---|---|---|---|---|
| 01 June | Balance b/d | 550 | 07 June | 110123 | Connell | 430 |
| 09 June | Cash sales | 840 | 07 June | 110124 | Renner | 720 |
| 14 June | Cash sales | 1,540 | 07 June | 110125 | Bond | 750 |
| 22 June | Cunnington | 1,730 | 07 June | 110126 | Hatton | 75 |
| | | | 07 June | 110127 | Bull | 270 |
| | | | 07 June | 110128 | Black | 135 |
| | | | 07 June | 110129 | Southall | 740 |
| | | | | | | |
| | | | | | | |
| | | | | | | |
| | | | | | | |
| | | | | | | |
| | | | | | | |

(a)    Check the items on the bank statement against the items in the cash book.

(b)    Enter any items in the cash book as needed.

(c)    Total the cash book and clearly show the balance carried down at 23 June (closing balance) and brought down at 24 June (opening balance).

## 58    MCKEOWN

The bank statement and cash book for McKeown is shown below.

| | Money Bags Bank PLC | | | | |
|---|---|---|---|---|---|
| To: McKeown Ltd | Account No: 47013799 | | 23 June 20XX | | |
| | **Statement of Account** | | | | |
| Date 20XX | Detail | Paid out £ | Paid in £ | Balance £ | |
| 01 June | Balance b/d | | | 7,420 | C |
| 01 June | Bank Giro Credit Pond | | 180 | 7,600 | C |
| 01 June | Cheque 110156 | 420 | | 7,180 | C |
| 01 June | Interest received | | 85 | 7,265 | C |
| 11 June | Cheque 110157 | 430 | | 6,835 | C |
| 12 June | Cheque 110158 | 520 | | 6,315 | C |
| 13 June | Cheque 110161 | 750 | | 5,565 | C |
| 15 June | Bank Giro Credit Sherwood | | 640 | 6,205 | C |
| 17 June | Paid in to Money Bags Bank | | 1,200 | 7,405 | C |
| 20 June | Bank Giro Credit Coyne | | 1,630 | 9,035 | C |
| 23 June | Direct debit Wilmott | 300 | | 8,735 | C |
| 23 June | Interest received | | 35 | 8,770 | C |
| | D = Debit   C = Credit | | | | |

**Cash book**

| Date 20XX | Details | Bank £ | Date 20XX | Cheque number | Details | Bank £ |
|---|---|---|---|---|---|---|
| 01 June | Balance b/d | 7,180 | 07 June | 110157 | Williams | 430 |
| 12 June | Sherwood | 640 | 07 June | 110158 | Forecast | 520 |
| 14 June | Cash sales | 1,200 | 07 June | 110159 | Beasant | 1,240 |
| 22 June | Tweedy | 860 | 07 June | 110160 | Davison | 1,420 |
| 23 June | Butterwood | 440 | 07 June | 110161 | Mildenhall | 750 |
| | | | | | | |
| | | | | | | |
| | | | | | | |
| | | | | | | |
| | | | | | | |
| | | | | | | |
| | | | | | | |
| | | | | | | |

(a)    Check the items on the bank statement against the items in the cash book.

(b)    Enter any items in the cash book as needed.

(c)    Total the cash book and clearly show the balance carried down at 23 June (closing balance) and brought down at 24 June (opening balance).

## BANK RECONCILIATIONS

### 59    RIVERS BANK RECONCILIATION

Below is the bank statement and **updated** cash book for Rivers.

| Midway Bank PLC | | | | |
|---|---|---|---|---|
| **52 The Parade, Middleton, MD1 9LA** | | | | |
| To: Rivers Ltd | Account No: 28012877 | | 23 June 20XX | |
| **Statement of Account** | | | | |
| **Date** | **Detail** | **Paid out** | **Paid in** | **Balance** |
| **20XX** | | £ | £ | £ |
| 04 June | Balance b/d | | | 3,115 C |
| 04 June | Cheque 101013 | 650 | | 2,465 C |
| 04 June | Cheque 101014 | 1,420 | | 1,045 C |
| 05 June | Cheque 101015 | 60 | | 985 C |
| 07 June | Cheque 101018 | 450 | | 535 C |
| 12 June | Bank Giro Credit Ayreshire Build | | 970 | 1,505 C |
| 13 June | Cheque 101016 | 615 | | 890 C |
| 15 June | Direct debit Collins | 175 | | 715 C |
| 17 June | Paid in at Midway bank | | 300 | 1,015 C |
| 20 June | Direct Debit rent | 500 | | 515 C |
| 23 June | Bank interest | | 15 | 530 C |
| 23 June | Bank charges | 20 | | 510 C |
| D = Debit   C = Credit | | | | |

| Date 20XX | Details | Bank £ | Date 20XX | Cheque number | Details | Bank £ |
|---|---|---|---|---|---|---|
| 01 June | Balance b/d | 3,115 | 01 June | 101013 | Indigo Beds | 650 |
| 17 June | Bracken Ltd | 300 | 01 June | 101014 | DirectFit | 1,420 |
| 21 June | Airfleet Interiors | 560 | 01 June | 101015 | Langdon | 60 |
| 22 June | Harris Homes | 333 | 01 June | 101016 | QPF Ltd | 615 |
| 12 June | Ayreshire Build | 970 | 02 June | 101017 | OMD Ltd | 815 |
| 23 June | Bank Interest | 15 | 02 June | 101018 | Hamden Ltd | 450 |
| | | | 13 June | 101019 | Freeman & Cope | 522 |
| | | | 13 June | | Collins | 175 |
| | | | 20 June | | Rent | 500 |
| | | | 23 June | | Bank charges | 20 |
| | | | 23 June | | Balance c/d | 66 |
| | | 5,293 | | | | 5,293 |
| 24 June | Balance b/d | 66 | | | | |

**Complete the bank reconciliation statement as at 23 June.**

**Note:** Do not make any entries in the shaded boxes.

**Bank reconciliation statement as at 23 June 20XX**

| Balance per bank statement | £ |
|---|---|
| Add: | |
| Name: | £ |
| Name: | £ |
| Total to add | £ |
| Less: | |
| Name: | £ |
| Name: | £ |
| Total to subtract | £ |
| Balance as per cash book | £ |

Name options: Bank charges, QPF Ltd, Bracken Ltd, Ayreshire Build, Directfit, Hamden Ltd, Rent, Collins, Langdon, Airfleet Interiors, Freeman and Cope, OMD Ltd, Bank interest, Indigo Beds, Harris homes.

## 60    LUXURY BATHROOMS BANK RECONCILIATION

Below is the bank statement and updated cash book for Luxury Bathrooms.

| | | | | |
|---|---|---|---|---|
| **SKB Bank plc** | | | | |
| **68 London Road, Reading, RG8 4RN** | | | | |
| To:  Luxury Bathrooms | Account No: 55548921 | | 24 April 20XX | |

**Statement of Account**

| Date | Detail | Paid out | Paid in | Balance | |
|---|---|---|---|---|---|
| 20XX | | £ | £ | £ | |
| 03 April | Balance b/d | | | 17,845 | C |
| 03 April | Cheque 120045 | 8,850 | | 8,995 | C |
| 04 April | Bank Giro Ricketts & Co | | 465 | 9,460 | C |
| 04 April | Cheque 120046 | 2,250 | | 7,210 | C |
| 05 April | Cheque 120047 | 64 | | 7,146 | C |
| 08 April | Cheque 120048 | 3,256 | | 3,890 | C |
| 14 April | Direct Debit AMB Ltd | 2,265 | | 1,625 | C |
| 14 April | Direct Debit D Draper | 2,950 | | 1,325 | D |
| 14 April | Cheque 120050 | 655 | | 1,980 | D |
| 22 April | Paid in at SKB Bank | | 2,150 | 170 | C |
| 22 April | Bank charges | 63 | | 107 | C |
| 23 April | Overdraft fee | 25 | | 82 | C |
| D = Debit    C = Credit | | | | | |

| Date | Details | Bank | Date | Cheque | Details | Bank |
|---|---|---|---|---|---|---|
| 01 April | Balance b/d | 17,845 | 01 April | 120045 | R Sterling Ltd | 8,850 |
| 19 April | Olsen & Lane | 2,150 | 01 April | 120046 | Bert Cooper | 2,250 |
| 22 April | Frith Ltd | 685 | 01 April | 120047 | Hetko & Sons | 64 |
| 22 April | Hodgetts & Co | 282 | 02 April | 120048 | Barrett Ltd | 3,256 |
| 04 April | Ricketts & Co | 465 | 02 April | 120049 | K Plomer | 542 |
| | | | 08 April | 120050 | I&E Brown | 655 |
| | | | 08 April | 120051 | T Roberts | 1,698 |
| | | | 14 April | | AMB Ltd | 2,265 |
| | | | 14 April | | D Draper | 2,950 |
| | | | 22 April | | Bank charges | 63 |
| | | | 23 April | | Overdraft fee | 25 |
| 24 April | Balance c/d | 1,191 | | | | |
| | | 22,618 | | | | 22,618 |
| | | | 25 April | | Balance b/d | 1,191 |

Complete the bank reconciliation statement as at 24 April.

**Note:** Do not make any entries in the shaded boxes.

**Bank reconciliation statement as at 24 April 20XX.**

| Balance per bank statement | £ |
|---|---|
| Add: | |
| Name: | £ |
| Name: | £ |
| Total to add | £ |
| Less: | |
| Name: | £ |
| Name: | £ |
| Total to subtract | £ |
| Balance as per cash book | £ |

Name options: Bank charges, , R Sterling Ltd, Olsen & Lane, Frith Ltd, Hodgetts & Co, Bert Cooper, Hetko & Sons, Barrett Ltd, K Plomer, I&E Brown, T Roberts, AMB Ltd, Ricketts & Co, D Draper, Overdraft fee.

## 61  WHOLESALE FLOORING BANK RECONCILIATION

Below is the bank statement and updated cash book for Wholesale Flooring.

**Money Bags Bank PLC**
**52 Oak Road, Timperley, SK10 8LR**

To: Wholesale Flooring          Account No: 47013799          23 June 20XX
**Statement of Account**

| Date | Detail | Paid out | Paid in | Balance | |
|---|---|---|---|---|---|
| 20XX | | £ | £ | £ | |
| 04 June | Balance b/d | | | 5,125 | D |
| 05 June | Cheque 104373 | 890 | | 6,015 | D |
| 05 June | Cheque 104374 | 1,725 | | 7,740 | D |
| 05 June | Cheque 104375 | 210 | | 7,950 | D |
| 11 June | Cheque 104378 | 784 | | 8,734 | D |
| 12 June | Bank Giro Credit Aintree and Co | | 1,250 | 7,484 | D |
| 13 June | Cheque 104376 | 1,275 | | 8,759 | D |
| 15 June | Cheque 104377 | 725 | | 9,484 | D |
| 17 June | Paid in at Money Bags Bank plc | | 550 | 8,934 | D |
| 20 June | Direct debit MD County Council | 400 | | 9,334 | D |
| 23 June | Bank charges | 160 | | 9,494 | D |
| 23 June | Overdraft fee | 90 | | 9,584 | D |
| | D = Debit   C = Credit | | | | |

| Date 20XX | Details | Bank £ | Date 20XX | Cheque number | Details | Bank £ |
|---|---|---|---|---|---|---|
| | | | 01 June | | Balance b/d | 5,125 |
| 16 June | Beeston's | 550 | 01 June | 104373 | Good Iron | 890 |
| 19 June | Airfleet Exteriors | 3,025 | 01 June | 104374 | Ashworth & Co | 1,725 |
| 22 June | Jones's | 2,775 | 01 June | 104375 | Ironfit | 210 |
| 12 June | Aintree & Co | 1,250 | 05 June | 104376 | OSS Ltd | 1,275 |
| | | | 07 June | 104377 | Perfect Tools | 725 |
| | | | 08 June | 104378 | Campden Ltd | 784 |
| | | | 14 June | 104379 | Thornley & Thwaite | 675 |
| | | | 14 June | 104380 | Castle and Cove | 178 |
| | | | 20 June | | MD County Council | 400 |
| | | | 23 June | | Bank charges | 160 |
| 23 June | Balance c/d | 4,637 | 23 June | | Overdraft fee | 90 |
| | | 12,237 | | | | 12,237 |
| | | | 24 June | | Balance b/d | 4,637 |

**Complete the bank reconciliation statement as at 23 June.**

**Note:** Do not make any entries in the shaded boxes.

**Bank reconciliation statement as at 23 June 20XX**

| Balance per bank statement | £ |
|---|---|
| Add: | |
| Name: | £ |
| Name: | £ |
| Total to add | £ |
| Less: | |
| Name: | £ |
| Name: | £ |
| Total to subtract | £ |
| Balance as per cash book | £ |

Name options: Bank charges, OSS Ltd, Beeston's, Aintree and Co, Ironfit, Campden Ltd, MD County Council, Ashworth & Co, Airfleet Exteriors, Thornley & Thwaite, Perfect Tools, Overdraft fee, Castle & Cove, Good Iron, Jones's.

## 62    24 HOUR TAXIS BANK RECONCILIATION

Below is the bank statement and updated cash book for 24 Hour Taxis.

| | Four Kings Bank PLC | | | | |
|---|---|---|---|---|---|
| | **124 Four Kings Way, Newton Mearns, GL10 5QR** | | | | |
| To: 24 Hour Taxis | | Account No: 16135844 | | 23 June 20XX | |
| | | **Statement of Account** | | | |
| **Date** | **Detail** | **Paid out** | **Paid in** | **Balance** | |
| **20XX** | | £ | £ | £ | |
| 04 June | Balance b/d | | | 6,025 | C |
| 05 June | Cheque 102597 | 910 | | 5,115 | C |
| 05 June | Cheque 102598 | 2,010 | | 3,105 | C |
| 05 June | Cheque 102599 | 315 | | 2,790 | C |
| 11 June | Cheque 102602 | 675 | | 2,115 | C |
| 12 June | Bank Giro credit Barron Homes | | 1,475 | 3,590 | C |
| 13 June | Cheque 102600 | 1,725 | | 1,865 | C |
| 15 June | Cheque 102601 | 686 | | 1,179 | C |
| 18 June | Paid in at Four Kings Bank | | 1,000 | 2,179 | C |
| 20 June | Direct Debit AB Insurance | 1,250 | | 929 | C |
| 23 June | Bank charges | 50 | | 879 | C |
| 23 June | Overdraft fee | 25 | | 854 | C |
| | D = Debit    C = Credit | | | | |

| Date 20XX | Details | Bank £ | Date 20XX | Cheque number | Details | Bank £ |
|---|---|---|---|---|---|---|
| 01 June | Balance b/d | 6,025 | 01 June | 102597 | Best ideas | 910 |
| 18 June | Earnshaw's | 1,000 | 02 June | 102598 | Bentley and Burn | 2,010 |
| 19 June | Mainstreet Ltd | 1,206 | 02 June | 102599 | Bits and Bats | 315 |
| 21 June | Housley Inc | 1,725 | 03 June | 102600 | LPF Ltd | 1,725 |
| 12 June | Barron Homes | 1,475 | 07 June | 102601 | Essentials | 686 |
| | | | 08 June | 102602 | Hopburn Ltd | 675 |
| | | | 15 June | 102603 | Thistle Tools | 410 |
| | | | 15 June | 102604 | C Campbell Ltd | 275 |
| | | | 20 June | | AB Insurance | 1,250 |
| | | | 23 June | | Bank charges | 50 |
| | | | 23 June | | Overdraft fee | 25 |
| | | | 23 June | | Balance c/d | 3,100 |
| | | 11,431 | | | | 11,431 |
| 24 June | Balance b/d | 3,100 | | | | |

Complete the bank reconciliation statement as at 23 June.

**Note:** Do not make any entries in the shaded boxes.

**Bank reconciliation statement as at 23 June 20XX**

| Balance per bank statement | £ |
|---|---|
| Add: | |
| Name: | £ |
| Name: | £ |
| Total to add | £ |
| Less: | |
| Name: | £ |
| Name: | £ |
| Total to subtract | £ |
| Balance as per cash book | £ |

Name options: Bank charges, LPF Ltd, Earnshaw's, Barron Homes, Best Ideas, C Campbell Ltd, AB Insurance, Housley Inc, Mainstreet Ltd, Thistle Tools, Bentley and Burn, Overdraft fee, Hopburn Ltd, Bits & Bats, Essentials.

## 63   WOOD BANK RECONCILIATION

The bank statement and cash book for Wood is shown below.

**Money Bags Bank PLC**
**52 Oak Road, Timperley, SK10 8LR**

To: Wood Ltd                Account No: 47013799                23 June 20XX
**Statement of Account**

| Date 20XX | Detail | Paid out £ | Paid in £ | Balance £ | |
|---|---|---|---|---|---|
| 04 June | Balance b/d | | | 17,640 | C |
| 05 June | Bank Giro Credit Bradley | | 1,320 | 18,960 | C |
| 05 June | Bank Giro Credit Thanoj | | 2,450 | 21,410 | C |
| 05 June | Paid in at Money Bags Bank PLC | | 9,420 | 30,830 | C |
| 11 June | Cheque 110341 | 1,540 | | 29,290 | C |
| 12 June | BACS payment Southwell | 820 | | 28,470 | C |
| 13 June | Cheque 110343 | 750 | | 27,720 | C |
| 15 June | Cheque 110344 | 570 | | 27,150 | C |
| 17 June | Interest earned | | 80 | 27,230 | C |
| 20 June | Direct Debit Blundell | 400 | | 26,830 | C |
| 23 June | BACS payment Bore | 250 | | 26,580 | C |
| 23 June | Cheque 110346 | 740 | | 25,840 | C |
| | D = Debit   C = Credit | | | | |

**Cash book**

| Date 20XX | Details | Bank £ | Date 20XX | Cheque number | Details | Bank £ |
|---|---|---|---|---|---|---|
| 01 June | Balance b/d | 17,640 | | | | |
| 03 June | Bradley | 1,320 | 04 June | 110341 | Carr | 1,540 |
| 03 June | Cash sales | 9,420 | 04 June | 110342 | Ramsden | 980 |
| 03 June | Thanoj | 2,450 | 04 June | 110343 | Coulson | 750 |
| 21 June | Cash sales | 7,430 | 04 June | 110344 | Brodie | 570 |
| 21 June | Devitt | 1,990 | 04 June | 110345 | Jones | 550 |
| 17 June | Interest earned | 80 | 04 June | 110346 | Gritton | 740 |
| | | | 20 June | | Bore | 250 |
| | | | 12 June | | Southwell | 820 |
| | | | 20 June | | Direct Debit Blundell | 400 |
| | | | | | | |
| | | | | | | |
| | | | | | | |

(a) Complete the bank reconciliation statement as at **23 June**.

**Note:** Do not make any entries in the shaded boxes.

**Bank reconciliation statement as at 23 June 20XX**

| | |
|---|---|
| Balance per bank statement | |
| Add: | |
| Name: | |
| Name: | |
| Total to add | |
| Less: | |
| Name: | |
| Name: | |
| Total to subtract | |
| Balance as per cash book | |

(b) Refer to the cash book in (a) and check that the bank statement has correctly been reconciled by calculating:

– The balance carried down

– The total of each of the bank columns after the balance carried down has been recorded

| Balance carried down £ | Bank column totals £ |
|---|---|
| | |

## 64   PEARSON BANK RECONCILIATION

The bank statement and cash book for Pearson is shown below.

**Money Bags Bank PLC**

To: Pearson Ltd                Account No: 47013799                23 June 20XX

**Statement of Account**

| Date 20XX | Detail | Paid out £ | Paid in £ | Balance £ | |
|---|---|---|---|---|---|
| 01 June | Balance b/d | | | 1,340 | D |
| 02 June | Bank Giro Credit Pond | | 1,890 | 550 | C |
| 02 June | Interest received | | 5 | 555 | C |
| 02 June | Direct Debit McMenemy | 1,200 | | 645 | D |
| 11 June | Cheque 110123 | 430 | | 1,075 | D |
| 12 June | Paid in to Money Bags Bank | | 840 | 235 | D |
| 13 June | Cheque 110126 | 75 | | 310 | D |
| 15 June | Cheque 110127 | 270 | | 580 | D |
| 17 June | Paid in to Money Bags bank | | 1,540 | 960 | C |
| 20 June | Direct Debit Findus | 300 | | 660 | C |
| 23 June | Bank charges | 25 | | 635 | C |
| 23 June | Cheque 110129 | 740 | | 105 | D |

D = Debit   C = Credit

**Cash book**

| Date 20XX | Details | Bank £ | Date 20XX | Cheque number | Details | Bank £ |
|---|---|---|---|---|---|---|
| 01 June | Balance b/d | 550 | 07 June | 110123 | Connell | 430 |
| 09 June | Cash sales | 840 | 07 June | 110124 | Renner | 720 |
| 14 June | Cash sales | 1,540 | 07 June | 110125 | Bond | 750 |
| 22 June | Cunnington | 1,730 | 07 June | 110126 | Hatton | 75 |
| 02 June | Interest received | 5 | 07 June | 110127 | Bull | 270 |
| | | | 07 June | 110128 | Black | 135 |
| | | | 07 June | 110129 | Southall | 740 |
| | | | 02 June | | McMenemy | 1,200 |
| | | | 20 June | | Findus | 300 |
| | | | 23 June | | Bank charges | 25 |
| | | | 23 June | | Balance c/d | 20 |
| | | 4,665 | | | | 4,665 |
| 24 June | Balance b/d | 20 | | | | |

(a) **Complete the bank reconciliation statement as at 23 June.**

**Note:** Do not make any entries in the shaded boxes.

**Bank reconciliation statement as at 23 June 20XX**

| Balance per bank statement | |
|---|---|
| Add: | |
| Name: | |
| Total to add | |
| Less: | |
| Name: | |
| Name: | |
| Name: | |
| Total to subtract | |
| Balance as per cash book | |

(b) **Show which security procedure listed below Pearson should use to ensure the security of receipts from customers.**

| | ✓ |
|---|---|
| Cash received from customers should be kept in a locked safe until banked | |
| Cash should be banked on a monthly basis | |
| Cheques received too late to bank should be posted through the bank's letter box | |

## 65    MCKEOWN BANK RECONCILIATION

The bank statement and cash book for McKeown is shown below.

### Money Bags Bank PLC

| To: McKeown Ltd | Account No: 47013799 | | 23 June 20XX | |

#### Statement of Account

| Date | Detail | Paid out | Paid in | Balance | |
|------|--------|----------|---------|---------|---|
| **20XX** | | £ | £ | £ | |
| 01 June | Balance b/d | | | 7,420 | C |
| 01 June | Bank Giro Credit Pond | | 180 | 7,600 | C |
| 01 June | Cheque 110156 | 420 | | 7,180 | C |
| 01 June | Interest received | | 85 | 7,265 | C |
| 11 June | Cheque 110157 | 430 | | 6,835 | C |
| 12 June | Cheque 110158 | 520 | | 6,315 | C |
| 13 June | Cheque 110161 | 750 | | 5,565 | C |
| 15 June | Bank Giro Credit Sherwood | | 640 | 6,205 | C |
| 17 June | Paid in to Money Bags Bank | | 1,200 | 7,405 | C |
| 20 June | Bank Giro Credit Coyne | | 1,630 | 9,035 | C |
| 23 June | Direct Debit Wilmott | 300 | | 8,735 | C |
| 23 June | Interest received | | 35 | 8,770 | C |
| | **D = Debit    C = Credit** | | | | |

### Cash book

| Date 20XX | Details | Bank £ | Date 20XX | Cheque number | Details | Bank £ |
|-----------|---------|--------|-----------|---------------|---------|--------|
| 01 June | Balance b/d | 7,180 | 07 June | 110157 | Williams | 430 |
| 12 June | Sherwood | 640 | 07 June | 110158 | Forecast | 520 |
| 14 June | Cash sales | 1,200 | 07 June | 110159 | Beasant | 1,240 |
| 22 June | Tweedy | 860 | 07 June | 110160 | Davison | 1,420 |
| 23 June | Butterwood | 440 | 07 June | 110161 | Mildenhall | 750 |
| 01 June | Interest received | 85 | 23 June | | Wilmott | 300 |
| 20 June | Coyne | 1,630 | | | | |
| 23 June | Interest received | 35 | | | | |
| | | | | | | |
| | | | | | | |
| | | | | | | |

(a)   Complete the bank reconciliation statement as at 23 June.

Note: Do not make any entries in the shaded boxes.

Bank reconciliation statement as at 23 June 20XX

| | |
|---|---|
| Balance per bank statement | |
| Add: | |
| Name: | |
| Name: | |
| Total to add | |
| Less: | |
| Name: | |
| Name: | |
| Total to subtract | |
| Balance as per cash book | |

(b)   Refer to the cash book in (a) and check that the bank statement has correctly been reconciled by calculating:

–   the balance carried down

–   the total of each of the bank columns after the balance carried down has been recorded.

| Balance carried down £ | Bank column totals £ |
|---|---|
| | |

# PREPARE AND RECONCILE SALES/PURCHASE LEDGER CONTROL ACCOUNTS

## 66   MONSTER MUNCHIES

This is a summary of transactions with customers of Monster Munchies during the month of June.

(a)   Show whether each entry will be a debit or credit in the Sales ledger control account in the General ledger.

| Details | Amount £ | Debit ✓ | Credit ✓ |
|---|---|---|---|
| Balance of receivables at 1 June | 48,000 | | |
| Goods sold on credit | 12,415 | | |
| Receipts from credit customers | 22,513 | | |
| Discount allowed | 465 | | |
| Sales returns from credit customers | 320 | | |

**(b)**    **What will be the balance brought down on 1 July on the above account?**

✓

| | |
|---|---|
| Dr £37,117 | |
| Cr £37,117 | |
| Dr £83,713 | |
| Cr £83,713 | |
| Dr £58,883 | |
| Cr £58,883 | |

The following debit balances were in the subsidiary sales ledger on 1 July.

| | £ |
|---|---|
| XXX Ltd | 21,300 |
| Brittle Homes Ltd | 5,376 |
| Colin and Campbell | 333 |
| Bashford Incorporated | 1,733 |
| Mainstreet Homes | 3,426 |
| Shamrock Interiors | 4,629 |

**(c)**    **Reconcile the balances shown above with the sales ledger control account balance you have calculated in part (a).**

| | £ |
|---|---|
| Sales ledger control account balance as at 30 June | |
| Total of subsidiary sales ledger accounts as at 30 June | |
| Difference | |

**(d)**    **Which TWO of the following reasons could be explanations of why the total on a sales ledger control account may be higher than the total of balances on a sales ledger?**

✓

| | |
|---|---|
| Sales returns may have been omitted from the subsidiary ledger. | |
| Discounts allowed may have been omitted from the subsidiary ledger. | |
| Sales returns may have been entered in the subsidiary ledger twice. | |
| Discounts allowed may have been entered in the subsidiary ledger twice. | |

It is important to reconcile the sales ledger control account on a regular basis.

(e)    **Which of the following statements is true?**

| | ✓ |
|---|---|
| Reconciliation of the sales ledger control account assures managers that the amount showing as owed to suppliers is correct. | |
| Reconciliation of the sales ledger control account assures managers that the amount showing as outstanding from customers is correct. | |
| Reconciliation of the sales ledger control account will show if a purchase invoice has been omitted from the purchase ledger. | |
| Reconciliation of the sales ledger control account will show if a purchase invoice has been omitted from the sales ledger. | |

## 67    JACK'S BOX

This is a summary of transactions with customers of Jack's Box during the month of April.

(a)    **Show whether each entry will be a debit or a credit in the Sales ledger control account in the General ledger.**

| Details | Amount £ | Debit ✓ | Credit ✓ |
|---|---|---|---|
| Balance of receivables at 1 April | 60,589 | | |
| Goods sold on credit | 26,869 | | |
| Payments received from credit customers | 29,411 | | |
| Discount allowed | 598 | | |
| Goods returned from credit customers | 1,223 | | |

(b)    **What will be the balance brought down on 1 May on the above account?**

| | ✓ |
|---|---|
| Dr £55,030 | |
| Cr £55,030 | |
| Dr £56,226 | |
| Cr £56,226 | |
| Dr £52,584 | |
| Cr £52,584 | |

The following debit balances were in the subsidiary sales ledger on 1 May.

| | £ |
|---|---|
| Olsen & Lane | 19,455 |
| Frith Ltd | 625 |
| Hodgetts & Co | 412 |
| Geevor plc | 17,623 |
| Trevaskis Farm Ltd | 16,888 |

(c) **Reconcile the balances shown above with the sales ledger control account balance you have calculated in part (b).**

|  | £ |
|---|---|
| Sales ledger control account balances as at 30 April |  |
| Total of subsidiary sales ledger accounts as at 30 April |  |
| Difference |  |

(d) **What may have caused the difference of £1,223 you calculated in part (c)?**

|  | ✓ |
|---|---|
| Sales returns may have been omitted from the subsidiary ledger |  |
| Discounts allowed may have been omitted from the subsidiary ledger |  |
| Sales returns have been entered into the subsidiary ledger twice |  |
| Discounts allowed have been entered into subsidiary ledger twice |  |

It is important to reconcile the sales ledger control account on a regular basis.

(e) **Which of the following statements is true?**

|  | ✓ |
|---|---|
| Reconciliation of the sales ledger control account will show if a purchase invoice has been omitted from the purchases ledger. |  |
| Reconciliation of the sales ledger control account will show if a sales invoice has been omitted from the purchases ledger. |  |
| Reconciliation of the sales ledger control account assures managers that the amount showing due to suppliers is correct. |  |
| Reconciliation of the sales ledger control account assures managers that the amount showing due from customers is correct. |  |

## 68 CILLA'S SINKS

This is a summary of transactions with suppliers of Cilla's Sinks during the month of June.

(a) **Show whether each entry will be a debit or credit in the Purchase Ledger control account in the General Ledger.**

| Details | Amount £ | Debit ✓ | Credit ✓ |
|---|---|---|---|
| Balance of payables at 1 June | 52,150 |  |  |
| Goods bought on credit | 19,215 |  |  |
| Payments made to credit suppliers | 19,073 |  |  |
| Discount received | 284 |  |  |
| Goods returned to credit suppliers | 1,023 |  |  |

(b)     **What will be the balance brought down on 1 July on the above account?**

✓

| | |
|---|---|
| Dr £51,553 | |
| Cr £51,553 | |
| Dr £50,985 | |
| Cr £50,985 | |
| Dr £50,701 | |
| Cr £50,701 | |

The following credit balances were in the subsidiary purchase ledger on 1 July.

| | £ |
|---|---|
| BWF Ltd | 19,563 |
| All Parts Ltd | 10,207 |
| Hove Albion | 4,501 |
| Barton Groves | 6,713 |
| Cambridge Irons | 5,913 |
| Outside Arenas | 5,111 |

(c)     **Reconcile the balances shown above with the purchase ledger control account balance you have calculated in part (a).**

| | £ |
|---|---|
| Purchase ledger control account balance as at 30 June | |
| Total of subsidiary purchase ledger accounts as at 30 June | |
| Difference | |

It is important to reconcile the purchase ledger control account on a regular basis.

(d)     **What may have caused the difference calculated in part (c)?**

✓

| | |
|---|---|
| Goods returned may have been omitted from the subsidiary ledger. | |
| Discounts received may have been omitted from the subsidiary ledger. | |
| Goods returned may have been entered in the subsidiary ledger twice. | |
| Discounts received may have been entered into the subsidiary ledger twice. | |

(e)   **Which of the following statements is true?**

| | ✓ |
|---|---|
| Reconciliation of the purchase ledger control account will help to identify any supplier invoices that have been omitted in error. | |
| Reconciliation of the purchase ledger control account will show if a sales invoice has been omitted from the purchase ledger. | |
| Reconciliation of the purchase ledger control account will show if a sales invoice has been omitted from the sales ledger. | |
| Reconciliation of the purchase ledger control account will help to identify any discounts allowed that have been omitted in error. | |

## 69   VIK'S TRICKS

This is a summary of transactions with customers of Vik's Tricks during the month of June.

(a)   **Show whether each entry will be a debit or credit in the Sales ledger control account in the General ledger.**

| Details | Amount £ | Debit ✓ | Credit ✓ |
|---|---|---|---|
| Balance of receivables at 1 June | 58,120 | | |
| Goods sold on credit | 20,013 | | |
| Receipts from credit customers | 22,327 | | |
| Discount allowed | 501 | | |
| Sales returns from credit customers | 970 | | |

(b)   **What will be the balance brought down on 1 July on the above account?**

| | ✓ |
|---|---|
| Dr £58,963 | |
| Cr £58,963 | |
| Dr £57,277 | |
| Cr £57,277 | |
| Dr £54,335 | |
| Cr £54,335 | |

The following debit balances were in the subsidiary sales ledger on 1 July.

|  | £ |
|---|---|
| Woffel Homes | 21,026 |
| Perfect Rooms Ltd | 14,709 |
| Brighton Dwellings Ltd | 7,864 |
| Grosvenor Homes | 3,198 |
| Oxford Designs | 3,011 |
| Indoor Delights | 5,497 |

**(c)** **Reconcile the balances shown above with the sales ledger control account balance you have calculated in part (a).**

|  | £ |
|---|---|
| Sales ledger control account balance as at 30 June |  |
| Total of subsidiary sales ledger accounts as at 30 June |  |
| Difference |  |

**(d)** **Which TWO of the following reasons could be explanations of why the total on a sales ledger control account may be LOWER than the total of balances on a sales ledger?**

|  | ✓ |
|---|---|
| Discounts allowed may have been entered in the subsidiary ledger twice. |  |
| Discounts allowed may have been omitted from the subsidiary ledger. |  |
| Sales returns may have been entered in the subsidiary ledger twice. |  |
| Sales returns may have been omitted from the subsidiary ledger. |  |

It is important to reconcile the sales ledger control account on a regular basis.

**(e)** **Which of the following statements is true?**

|  | ✓ |
|---|---|
| Reconciliation of the sales ledger control account will help to identify any customer invoices that have been omitted in error. |  |
| Reconciliation of the sales ledger control account will show if a purchase invoice has been omitted from the sales ledger. |  |
| Reconciliation of the sales ledger control account will show if a purchase invoice has been omitted from the purchase ledger. |  |
| Reconciliation of the sales ledger control account will help to identify any discounts received that have been omitted in error. |  |

**70    ZHANG**

When Zhang came to reconcile his SLCA with his list of balances on the sales ledger, he found that they did not match. The SLCA had a balance of £65,830 and the list of balances totalled £65,090. Upon further investigation, he discovered that the following errors had been made:

1      The sales day book had been incorrectly totalled and had been overcast by £1,200.

2      A contra of £800 had been made in the SLCA, but had not been recorded in the sales ledger.

3      A credit note of £130 had been posted twice in the sales ledger.

4      A discount given of £210 had only been recorded in the sales ledger.

**(a)    Update the SLCA and list of balances to make sure that the two agree.**

**SLCA**

| Details | Amount £ | Details | Amount £ |
|---|---|---|---|
| Balance b/d | 65,830 | | |
| | | | |
| | | Balance c/d | |
| | | | |
| Balance b/d | | | |

**List of balances:**

| | £ |
|---|---|
| Total | 65,090 |
| | |
| | |
| Revised total | |

**(b)    Show whether the following statements are true or false:**

| | True ✓ | False ✓ |
|---|---|---|
| An aged trade receivables analysis is used when chasing customers for outstanding payments. | | |
| An aged trade receivables analysis is sent to credit customers when payments are being requested. | | |

## 71  HANDYSIDE

When Handyside came to reconcile his PLCA with his list of balances on the purchases ledger, he found that they did not match. The PLCA had a balance of £25,360 and the list of balances totalled £26,000. Upon further investigation, he discovered that the following errors had been made:

1   In the purchases ledger, a purchase of £2,400 (including VAT at 20%) had been entered at the net amount.

2   Returns of £350 had not been included in the purchases ledger.

3   An invoice for £600 plus VAT had not been posted in the PLCA yet.

4   Returns of £120 were missing from the PLCA.

5   An invoice for £340 had been entered into the purchases ledger as £430.

(a)   **Update the PLCA and list of balances to make sure that the two agree.**

**PLCA**

| Details | Amount £ | Details | Amount £ |
|---|---|---|---|
| | | Balance b/d | 25,360 |
| | | | |
| Balance c/d | | | |
| | | | |
| | | Balance b/d | |

**List of balances:**

| | £ |
|---|---|
| Total | 26,000 |
| | |
| | |
| | |
| Revised total | |

(b)   **Show whether the following statements are true or false:**

| | True ✓ | False ✓ |
|---|---|---|
| The purchases ledger control account enables a business to see how much is owed to individual suppliers | | |
| The purchases ledger control account total should reconcile to the total of the list of supplier balances in the purchases ledger | | |

# VAT CONTROL ACCOUNT

## 72    RING RING TELEPHONE

The following is an extract from Ring Ring Telephone's books of prime entry.

|  | | **Totals for quarter** | |
|---|---|---|---|
| **Sales day-book** | | **Purchases day-book** | |
| Net: | £153,000 | Net: | £81,000 |
| VAT: | £30,600 | VAT: | £16,200 |
| Gross: | £183,600 | Gross: | £97,200 |
| **Sales returns day-book** | | **Purchases returns day-book** | |
| Net: | £1,800 | Net: | £5,800 |
| VAT: | £360 | VAT: | £1,160 |
| Gross: | £2,160 | Gross: | £6,960 |
| **Cash book** | | | |
| Net cash sales: | £240 | | |
| VAT: | £48 | | |
| Gross cash sales: | £288 | | |

(a)    **What will be the entries in the VAT control account to record the VAT transactions in the quarter?**

**VAT control**

| Details | Amount £ | Details | Amount £ |
|---|---|---|---|
| | | | |
| | | | |
| | | | |
| | | | |
| | | | |
| | | | |

Picklist: Cash sales, Purchases, Purchases returns, Sales, Sales returns, VAT.

The VAT return has been completed and shows an amount owing from HMRC of £15,248.

(b)    **Is the VAT return correct?**   Yes/No

(c)   At the end of the next period, the VAT control account has debit entries amounting to £93,800 and credit entries amounting to £54,400.

The following transactions have not yet been recorded in the VAT control account:

VAT of £400 on purchase of equipment

VAT of £900 on cash sales

**What will be the balance brought down on the VAT account after the transactions above have been recorded? Also identify whether the balance will be a debit or a credit.**

| | £ | Debit | Credit |
|---|---|---|---|
| Balance brought down | | | |

## 73   JO'S JOINERS

The following is an extract from Jo's Joiners books of prime entry.

| Totals for quarter | | | |
|---|---|---|---|
| **Sales day book** | | **Purchases day book** | |
| Net: | £156,000 | Net: | £105,000 |
| VAT: | £31,200 | VAT: | £21,000 |
| Gross: | £187,200 | Gross: | £126,000 |
| **Sales returns day book** | | **Purchases returns day book** | |
| Net: | £3,600 | Net: | £5,440 |
| VAT: | £720 | VAT: | £1,088 |
| Gross: | £4,320 | Gross: | £6,528 |
| **Cash Book** | | | |
| Net cash sales: | £600 | | |
| VAT: | £120 | | |
| Gross cash sales: | £720 | | |

(a)   **What will be the entries in the VAT control account to record the VAT transactions in the quarter?**

**VAT Control**

| Details | Amount £ | Details | Amount £ |
|---|---|---|---|
| | | | |
| | | | |
| | | | |
| | | | |
| | | | |
| | | | |

Picklist: Cash sales, Purchases, Purchases returns, Sales, Sales returns, VAT.

The VAT return has been completed and shows an amount owed to HMRC of £10,688.

(b)   **Is the VAT return correct?**                         Yes/No

## 74    PHILIP'S CABINS

The following is an extract from Philip's Cabins books of prime entry.

| | Totals for quarter | | |
|---|---|---|---|
| **Sales day-book** | | **Purchases day-book** | |
| Net: | £179,800 | Net: | £100,200 |
| VAT: | £35,960 | VAT: | £20,040 |
| Gross: | £215,760 | Gross: | £120,240 |
| **Sales returns day-book** | | **Purchases returns day-book** | |
| Net: | £3,000 | Net: | £5,720 |
| VAT: | £600 | VAT: | £1,144 |
| Gross: | £3,600 | Gross: | £6,864 |
| **Cash book** | | | |
| Net cash sales: | £560 | | |
| VAT: | £112 | | |
| Gross cash sales: | £672 | | |

(a)    **What will be the entries in the VAT control account to record the VAT transactions in the quarter?**

### VAT control

| Details | Amount £ | Details | Amount £ |
|---|---|---|---|
| | | | |
| | | | |
| | | | |
| | | | |
| | | | |
| | | | |

Picklist:  Cash sales, Purchases, Purchases returns, Sales, Sales returns, VAT.

The VAT return has been completed and shows an amount due to HMRC of £14,540.

(b)    **Is the VAT return correct?**          Yes/No

## 75 DISLEY

(a) **Show whether each item is a debit or credit balance in the VAT control account by copying the amount into the correct column.**

| | £ | Debit | Credit |
|---|---|---|---|
| VAT total in the sales day book | 65,420 | | |
| VAT total in the purchases day book | 21,340 | | |
| VAT total in the sales returns day book | 480 | | |
| VAT balance brought forward, owed to HMRC | 24,910 | | |
| VAT on irrecoverable debts | 830 | | |
| VAT on petty cash expenses paid | 210 | | |

The VAT return has been completed and shows an amount due to HMRC of £67,740.

(b) **Is the VAT return correct?**  Yes/No

(c) At the end of the next period, the VAT control account has debit entries amounting to £42,300 and credit entries amounting to £61,250.

The following transactions have not yet been recorded in the VAT control account:

VAT total in the discounts received day book of £980

VAT of £200 on an irrecoverable debt

**What will be the balance brought down on the VAT account after the transactions above have been recorded? Also identify whether the balance will be a debit or a credit.**

| | £ | Debit | Credit |
|---|---|---|---|
| Balance brought down | | | |

## 76 KERR

(a) **Show whether each item is a debit or credit balance in the VAT control account by copying the amount into the correct column.**

| | £ | Debit | Credit |
|---|---|---|---|
| VAT total in the purchase returns day book | 1,320 | | |
| VAT total in discounts received day book | 400 | | |
| VAT on cash purchases | 2,670 | | |
| VAT on the sale of equipment | 970 | | |
| VAT total in discounts allowed day book | 500 | | |
| VAT refund received from HMRC | 2,580 | | |
| VAT on cash sales | 5,880 | | |
| VAT balance brought forward, due from HMRC | 2,580 | | |

The VAT return has been completed and shows an amount due to HMRC of £5,400.

(b) **Is the VAT return correct?**  Yes/No

## 77    NEILSON

(a)    Show whether each item is a debit or credit balance in the VAT control account by copying the amount into the correct column.

| | £ | Debit | Credit |
|---|---|---|---|
| VAT total in the sales day book | 54,670 | | |
| VAT total in the purchases day book | 26,340 | | |
| VAT total in the sales returns day book | 1,240 | | |
| VAT total in the purchases returns day book | 760 | | |
| VAT on sale of equipment | 3,210 | | |
| VAT on petty cash expenses paid | 500 | | |
| VAT balance brought forward, owed to HMRC | 42,180 | | |
| VAT on irrecoverable debts | 430 | | |
| VAT paid to HMRC during the period | 32,150 | | |
| VAT on cash sales | 6,540 | | |
| VAT on cash purchases | 7,520 | | |
| VAT total in discounts allowed day book | 1,130 | | |
| VAT total in discounts received day book | 980 | | |

The VAT return has been completed and shows an amount due to HMRC of £39,030.

(b)    **Is the VAT return correct?**  Yes/No

# THE BANKING SYSTEM

## 78    BLOSSOM BLOOMS

Blossom Blooms receives payment from customers and makes payments to suppliers in a variety of ways.

(a)    Select FOUR checks that DO NOT have to be made on each of the two payment methods shown below when received from customers.

| Checks to be made | Cheque ✓ | Telephone credit card payment ✓ |
|---|---|---|
| Check expiry date | | |
| Check issue number | | |
| Check not post dated | | |
| Check security number | | |
| Check words and figures match | | |
| Check card has not been tampered with | | |

(b)    **Show whether each of the statements below is true or false.**

When Blossom Blooms makes payments to suppliers by debit card, the amount paid affects the bank current account.

**True/False**

When Blossom Blooms makes payments to suppliers by credit card, the amount paid affects the bank current account.

**True/False**

## 79    PETE'S PARROTS

Pete's Parrots receives payment from customers and makes payments to suppliers in a variety of ways.

(a)    **Select TWO checks that have to be made on each of the two payment methods shown below when received from customers.**

| Checks to be made | Cheque ✔ | Telephone credit card payment ✔ |
|---|---|---|
| Check expiry date | | |
| Check issue number | | |
| Check not post dated | | |
| Check security number | | |
| Check words and figures match | | |
| Check card has not been tampered with | | |

(b)    **Show whether each of the statements below is true or false.**

When Pete's Parrots makes payments to suppliers by credit card, the amount does not leave the bank current account immediately.

**True/False**

When Pete's Parrots makes payments to suppliers by debit card, the amount paid affects the bank current account.

**True/False**

## 80    BANK EFFECTS 1

**Which TWO payments will NOT reduce funds in the bank balance of the payer at the date of payment?**

| | ✔ |
|---|---|
| Standing order | |
| Cheque payment | |
| CHAPS payment | |
| Credit card payment | |

## 81 BANK EFFECTS 2

**Which THREE payments WILL reduce funds in the bank balance of the payer at the date of payment?**

|  | ✓ |
|---|---|
| Direct debit |  |
| Building society cheque payment |  |
| Debit card payment |  |
| BACS payment |  |

## 82 METHODS OF PAYMENT 1

Match the payment need with the most likely method of payment to be used.

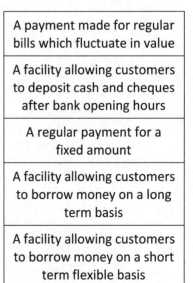

| | |
|---|---|
| Replacement batteries for office clock | CHAPS payment |
| Payment to complete the purchase of a new building, which needs to clear today | Debit/Credit card |
| Fixed monthly charge for rent | Direct debit |
| Payment for telephone bill, which fluctuates monthly | Cheque |
| Payment to regular supplier | Petty cash |
| Online purchase of computer equipment | Standing order |

## 83 METHODS OF PAYMENT 2

Match the payment with the description below

| | |
|---|---|
| Standing order | A payment made for regular bills which fluctuate in value |
| Bank loan | A facility allowing customers to deposit cash and cheques after bank opening hours |
| Direct debit | A regular payment for a fixed amount |
| Bank overdraft | A facility allowing customers to borrow money on a long term basis |
| Night safe | A facility allowing customers to borrow money on a short term flexible basis |

# Section 2

# ANSWERS TO PRACTICE QUESTIONS

## THE JOURNAL

**1    INTREPID INTERIORS**

(a)

| Account name | Amount £ | Debit ✓ | Credit ✓ |
|---|---|---|---|
| Cash at bank | 7,250 | ✓ | |
| Bank Loan | 5,000 | | ✓ |
| Capital | 10,625 | | ✓ |
| Motor vehicles | 4,750 | ✓ | |
| Insurances | 575 | ✓ | |
| Stationery | 300 | ✓ | |
| Sundry expenses | 225 | ✓ | |
| Motor expenses | 135 | ✓ | |
| Advertising | 990 | ✓ | |
| Rent and rates | 1,400 | ✓ | |

(b)

| Recording of a contra |
|---|

**2    BEDROOM BITS**

(a)

| Account name | Amount £ | Debit ✓ | Credit ✓ |
|---|---|---|---|
| Cash | 325 | ✓ | |
| Cash at bank | 9,625 | ✓ | |
| Capital | 22,008 | | ✓ |
| Fixtures and fittings | 4,250 | ✓ | |
| Insurance | 1,050 | ✓ | |
| Loan from bank | 15,000 | | ✓ |
| Miscellaneous expenses | 413 | ✓ | |
| Motor vehicle | 19,745 | ✓ | |
| Office expenses | 350 | ✓ | |
| Rent and rates | 1,250 | ✓ | |

**(b)**

| Irrecoverable debt written off |
| --- |

## 3  GARDEN GATES

| Account name | Amount £ | Debit ✓ | Credit ✓ |
| --- | --- | --- | --- |
| Cash | 450 | ✓ | |
| Cash at bank | 11,125 | ✓ | |
| Capital | 28,941 | | ✓ |
| Plant and machinery | 5,050 | ✓ | |
| Insurance | 990 | ✓ | |
| Loan from bank | 12,500 | | ✓ |
| General office expenses | 378 | ✓ | |
| Motor vehicle | 20,755 | ✓ | |

# PAYROLL

## 4  IVANO

**(a)**

| | Amount £ |
| --- | --- |
| Net pay (2,400 − 480 − 245 − 80) | 1,595 |

**Note:** The net pay is the gross pay less all the EMPLOYEE'S deductions. Employer's NIC is not part of this calculation.

**(b)**

| | Amount £ |
| --- | --- |
| Wages and salaries (Employer's expense) (2,400 Gross pay + 255 Employer's NIC) | 2,655 |

**(c)**

| | Amount £ |
| --- | --- |
| Liabilities (HMRC and Pension) HMRC = 480 + 245 + 255 = 980 Pension = 80 | 1,060 |

## 5 ANNA

**(a)**

|  | Amount £ |
|---|---|
| Net pay (1,400 – 280 – 125 – 60) | 935 |

**Note:** The net pay is the gross pay less all the EMPLOYEE'S deductions. Employer's NIC is not part of this calculation.

**(b)**

|  | Amount £ |
|---|---|
| Wages and salaries (Employer's expense)<br><br>(1,400 Gross pay + 135 Employer's NIC + 70 Employer pension contributions) | 1,605 |

**(c)**

|  | Amount £ |
|---|---|
| Liabilities (HMRC and pension)<br>HMRC = 280 + 125 + 135 = 540<br>Pension = 130 | 670 |

## 6 GROSS PAY 1

| Item | Added to gross pay ✓ | Not added to gross pay ✓ |
|---|---|---|
| Trade Union subscription |  | ✓ |
| Employer's NIC | ✓ |  |
| Employee's Pension |  | ✓ |
| Employer's Pension | ✓ |  |
| Employee's NIC |  | ✓ |

The wages expense comprises the employee's gross pay plus any contributions made by the employer, in this case pension and NIC. Trade Union subscription would be deducted from the employee's gross pay and paid to the Trade Union.

**7    GROSS PAY 2**

| Item | Deducted from gross pay ✓ | Not deducted from gross pay ✓ |
|---|---|---|
| Employer's NIC | | ✓ |
| Commission | | ✓ |
| Employee's NIC | ✓ | |
| Employee pension contribution | ✓ | |
| PAYE | ✓ | |

Gross pay is the amount the employee has earned from working for the company and therefore includes commission. Employer's NIC is added to gross pay in order to calculate the total wages expense for the company.

**8    A POCKET FULL OF POSES**

(i)

| Account name | Amount £ | Debit ✓ | Credit ✓ |
|---|---|---|---|
| Wages expense | 17,755 | ✓ | |
| Wages control | 17,755 | | ✓ |

(ii)

| Account name | Amount £ | Debit ✓ | Credit ✓ |
|---|---|---|---|
| Wages control | 7,500 | ✓ | |
| HMRC | 7,500 | | ✓ |

(iii)

| Account name | Amount £ | Debit ✓ | Credit ✓ |
|---|---|---|---|
| Wages control | 8,405 | ✓ | |
| Bank | 8,405 | | ✓ |

(iv)

| Account name | Amount £ | Debit ✓ | Credit ✓ |
|---|---|---|---|
| Wages control | 1,850 | ✓ | |
| Pension | 1,850 | | ✓ |

**Proof** (not required to answer the question correctly):

**Wages control**

| | | | |
|---|---|---|---|
| HM Revenue and Customs | 7,500 | Wages expense | 17,755 |
| Bank | 8,405 | | |
| Pension | 1,850 | | |
| | 17,755 | | 17,755 |

**9    RHYME TIME**

(i)

| Account name | Amount £ | Debit ✓ | Credit ✓ |
|---|---|---|---|
| Wages expense | 11,915 | ✓ | |
| Wages control | 11,915 | | ✓ |

(ii)

| Account name | Amount £ | Debit ✓ | Credit ✓ |
|---|---|---|---|
| Wages control | 5,026 | ✓ | |
| HMRC | 5,026 | | ✓ |

(iii)

| Account name | Amount £ | Debit ✓ | Credit ✓ |
|---|---|---|---|
| Wages control | 5,739 | ✓ | |
| Bank | 5,739 | | ✓ |

(iv)

| Account name | Amount £ | Debit ✓ | Credit ✓ |
|---|---|---|---|
| Wages control | 1,150 | ✓ | |
| Pension | 1,150 | | ✓ |

**Proof** (not required to answer the question correctly):

**Wages control**

| | | | |
|---|---|---|---|
| HMRC | 5,026 | Wages expense | 11,915 |
| Bank | 5,739 | | |
| Pension | 1,150 | | |
| | 11,915 | | 11,915 |

**10    DOWN & OUT**

(i)

| Account name | Amount £ | Debit ✓ | Credit ✓ |
|---|---|---|---|
| Wages expense | 9,567 | ✓ | |
| Wages control | 9,567 | | ✓ |

(ii)

| Account name | Amount £ | Debit ✓ | Credit ✓ |
|---|---|---|---|
| Wages control | 3,673 | ✓ | |
| HMRC | 3,673 | | ✓ |

(iii)

| Account name | Amount £ | Debit ✓ | Credit ✓ |
|---|---|---|---|
| Wages control | 5,469 | ✓ | |
| Bank | 5,469 | | ✓ |

(iv)

| Account name | Amount £ | Debit ✓ | Credit ✓ |
|---|---|---|---|
| Wages control | 425 | ✓ | |
| Trade union | 425 | | ✓ |

**Proof** (not required to answer the question correctly):

**Wages control**

| | | | |
|---|---|---|---|
| HMRC | 3,673 | Wages expense | 9,567 |
| Bank | 5,469 | | |
| Trade union | 425 | | |
| | ‾‾‾‾ | | ‾‾‾‾ |
| | 9,567 | | 9,567 |
| | ‾‾‾‾ | | ‾‾‾‾ |

**11    DEV**

(i)

| Account name | Amount £ | Debit ✓ | Credit ✓ |
|---|---|---|---|
| Wages expense | 13,963 | ✓ | |
| Wages control | 13,963 | | ✓ |

(ii)

| Account name | Amount £ | Debit ✓ | Credit ✓ |
|---|---|---|---|
| Wages control | 6,251 | ✓ | |
| HMRC | 6,251 | | ✓ |

(iii)

| Account name | Amount £ | Debit ✓ | Credit ✓ |
|---|---|---|---|
| Wages control | 7,212 | ✓ | |
| Bank | 7,212 | | ✓ |

(iv)

| Account name | Amount £ | Debit ✓ | Credit ✓ |
|---|---|---|---|
| Wages control | 500 | ✓ | |
| Trade union | 500 | | ✓ |

**Proof** (not required to answer the question correctly):

Wages control

| | | | |
|---|---|---|---|
| HMRC | 6,251 | Wages expense | 13,963 |
| Bank | 7,212 | | |
| Trade Union | 500 | | |
| | ——— | | ——— |
| | 13,963 | | 13,963 |
| | ——— | | ——— |

# IRRECOVERABLE DEBTS, CONTRAS AND TYPES OF ERROR

## 12 BEDROOM BITS 2

| Account name | Amount £ | Debit ✓ | Credit ✓ |
|---|---|---|---|
| Irrecoverable debts | 2,000 | ✓ | |
| VAT | 400 | ✓ | |
| Sales ledger control | 2,400 | | ✓ |

## 13 GARDEN GATES 2

| Account name | Amount £ | Debit ✓ | Credit ✓ |
|---|---|---|---|
| Irrecoverable debts | 2,600 | ✓ | |
| VAT | 520 | ✓ | |
| Sales ledger control | 3,120 | | ✓ |

## 14 CHESTNUT

### SLCA

| Details | Amount £ | Details | Amount £ |
|---|---|---|---|
| Balance b/d | 46,000 | Contra | 4,000 |
| | | Balance c/d | 42,000 |
| | **46,000** | | **46,000** |
| Balance b/d | 42,000 | | |

### PLCA

| Details | Amount £ | Details | Amount £ |
|---|---|---|---|
| Contra | 4,000 | Balance b/d | 31,000 |
| Balance c/d | 27,000 | | |
| | **31,000** | | **31,000** |
| | | Balance b/d | 27,000 |

## 15 ALLEN

### SLCA

| Details | Amount £ | Details | Amount £ |
|---|---|---|---|
| Balance b/d | 56,000 | Contra | 11,000 |
| | | Balance c/d | 45,000 |
| | **56,000** | | **56,000** |
| Balance b/d | 45,000 | | |

### PLCA

| Details | Amount £ | Details | Amount £ |
|---|---|---|---|
| Contra | 11,000 | Balance b/d | 49,000 |
| Balance c/d | 38,000 | | |
| | **49,000** | | **49,000** |
| | | Balance b/d | 38,000 |

## 16 BEANZ

| Account name | Amount £ | Debit ✓ | Credit ✓ |
|---|---|---|---|
| Irrecoverable debts | 4,350 | ✓ | |
| VAT | 870 | ✓ | |
| Sales ledger control | 5,220 | | ✓ |

## 17 ERROR TYPES 1

| Error in the general ledger | Error disclosed by the trial balance | Error NOT disclosed by the trial balance |
|---|---|---|
| Incorrectly calculating the balance on the Motor Vehicles account. | ✓ | |
| Recording a receipt for commission received in the bank interest received account. | | ✓ |
| Recording a bank receipt for bank interest received on the debit side of both the bank account and the bank interest received account. | ✓ | |
| Recording supplier invoices on the debit side of the purchase ledger control account and the credit side of the purchases account. | | ✓ |
| Recording a payment by cheque to a payable in the purchase ledger control account only. | ✓ | |
| Recording a bank payment of £124 for insurance as £142 in the insurance account and £124 in the bank account. | ✓ | |

## 18  ERROR TYPES 2

| Error in the general ledger | Would cause imbalance | Would NOT cause imbalance |
|---|---|---|
| Recording a bank receipt for rent received on the credit side of both the bank account and rent received account. | ✓ | |
| Recording a payment for new machinery in the equipment hire account. | | ✓ |
| Recording a purchase return on the credit side of the purchase ledger control account and the debit side of the purchase returns account. | | ✓ |
| Incorrectly calculating the balance on the bank interest received account. | ✓ | |
| Recording a payment by cheque to a payable in the bank account only. | ✓ | |
| Recording a bank payment of £120 for stationery as £210 in both accounts. | | ✓ |

## 19  ERROR TYPES 3

| Error in the general ledger | Type of error |
|---|---|
| Recording a bank receipt for rent received on the credit side of both the bank account and rent received account. | Two entries on one side |
| Recording a payment for new machinery in the equipment hire account. | Error of principle |
| Recording a purchase return on the credit side of the purchase ledger control account and the debit side of the purchase returns account. | Reversal of entries |

## 20  ERROR TYPES 4

| Error in the general ledger | Type of error |
|---|---|
| Recording a payment by cheque to a payable in the bank account only. | Single entry |
| Recording a bank payment of £100 for stationery as £210 in both accounts. | Error of original entry |
| Recording a receipt for commission received in the bank interest received account. | Error of commission |

**21    ERROR TYPES 5**

| Error in the general ledger | Type of error |
|---|---|
| A credit sale made at the month end was not recorded. | Error of omission |
| Recording a bank payment of £120 for stationery as £210 in the stationery account and correctly in the bank account. | Transposition error |
| Recording a receipt for commission received in the PLCA. | Error of principle |

**22    ERROR TYPES 6**

| Error in the general ledger | Would cause imbalance ✓ |
|---|---|
| Forgetting to post a journal to record a contra. | |
| Posting the VAT on a sale transaction as a debit rather than a credit. | ✓ |
| Recording a cash purchase in purchases and VAT only. | ✓ |
| Recording the electricity expense as a debit to wages expenses, with the corresponding entry correctly credited to cash. | |

**23    PRINCIPLES**

**(a)**

| Recording a bank payment for rent on the debit side of the office equipment account. | ✓ |
|---|---|

**(b)**

| Recording rent received as a debit in the rent account. | ✓ |
|---|---|

**24    EXTRACTION**

**(a)**

| Totalling the sales day book correctly but entering into the SLCA as a credit balance. | ✓ |
|---|---|

**(b)**

| Posting a £200 invoice for electricity as £210 in both the electricity and bank account. | ✓ |
|---|---|

# ERRORS

## 25 BANK ERROR

(i)

| Account name | Amount £ | Debit ✓ | Credit ✓ |
|---|---|---|---|
| Repairs | 750 | ✓ | |
| Bank | 750 | | ✓ |

(ii)

| Account name | Amount £ | Debit ✓ | Credit ✓ |
|---|---|---|---|
| Repairs | 750 | ✓ | |
| Bank | 750 | | ✓ |

## 26 RENT ERROR

(i)

| Account name | Amount £ | Debit ✓ | Credit ✓ |
|---|---|---|---|
| Bank | 500 | ✓ | |
| Rent received | 500 | | ✓ |

(ii)

| Account name | Amount £ | Debit ✓ | Credit ✓ |
|---|---|---|---|
| Bank | 500 | ✓ | |
| Rent received | 500 | | ✓ |

## 27 GAS ERROR

| Account name | Amount £ | Debit ✓ | Credit ✓ |
|---|---|---|---|
| Gas expenses | 300 | ✓ | |
| Electricity expenses | 300 | | ✓ |

## 28 BUILDING ERROR

| Account name | Amount £ | Debit ✓ | Credit ✓ |
|---|---|---|---|
| Suspense | 360,000 | ✓ | |
| Bank | 360,000 | | ✓ |

### 29 SALES ERROR

| Account name | Amount £ | Debit ✓ | Credit ✓ |
|---|---|---|---|
| Sales | 2,000 | ✓ | |
| VAT | 2,000 | | ✓ |

### 30 MOTOR ERROR

| Account name | Amount £ | Debit ✓ | Credit ✓ |
|---|---|---|---|
| Motor expenses | 700 | ✓ | |
| Motor vehicles | 700 | | ✓ |

### 31 INVENTORY ERROR

| Account name | Amount £ | Debit ✓ | Credit ✓ |
|---|---|---|---|
| Purchases | 375 | ✓ | |
| VAT | 75 | ✓ | |
| Purchase ledger control | 450 | | ✓ |

### 32 PLANT ERROR

| Account name | Amount £ | Debit ✓ | Credit ✓ |
|---|---|---|---|
| Depreciation expense | 24,000 | ✓ | |
| Accumulated depreciation | 24,000 | | ✓ |

### 33 PURCHASE ERROR

| Account name | Amount £ | Debit ✓ | Credit ✓ |
|---|---|---|---|
| VAT | 1,500 | ✓ | |
| Purchases | 1,500 | | ✓ |

### 34 INSURANCE ERROR

| Account name | Amount £ | Debit ✓ | Credit ✓ |
|---|---|---|---|
| Purchase ledger control | 2,700 | ✓ | |
| Bank | 2,700 | | ✓ |

# BALANCING THE TRIAL BALANCE AND CORRECTION OF ERRORS

## 35 CB INTERIORS

(i)

| Account name | Amount £ | Debit ✓ | Credit ✓ |
|---|---|---|---|
| Purchase ledger control | 960 | ✓ | |

(ii)

| Account name | Amount £ | Debit ✓ | Credit ✓ |
|---|---|---|---|
| Purchase ledger control | 9,600 | | ✓ |

(iii)

| Account name | Amount £ | Debit ✓ | Credit ✓ |
|---|---|---|---|
| Suspense | 8,640 | ✓ | |

## 36 ROGER DODGER

(i)

| Account name | Amount £ | Debit ✓ | Credit ✓ |
|---|---|---|---|
| VAT | 1,680 | ✓ | |

(ii)

| Account name | Amount £ | Debit ✓ | Credit ✓ |
|---|---|---|---|
| VAT | 1,320 | | ✓ |

(iii)

| Account name | Amount £ | Debit ✓ | Credit ✓ |
|---|---|---|---|
| Suspense | 360 | | ✓ |

## 37 A CUT ABOVE

(i)

| Account name | Amount £ | Debit ✓ | Credit ✓ |
|---|---|---|---|
| Purchase ledger control | 6,182 | | ✓ |

(ii)

| Account name | Amount £ | Debit ✓ | Credit ✓ |
|---|---|---|---|
| Purchase ledger control | 5,952 | ✓ | |

(iii)

| Account name | Amount £ | Debit ✓ | Credit ✓ |
|---|---|---|---|
| Suspense | 230 | ✓ | |

## 38 RESTCO

(i)

| Account name | Amount £ | Debit ✓ | Credit ✓ |
|---|---|---|---|
| Sales | 8,080 | ✓ | |

(ii)

| Account name | Amount £ | Debit ✓ | Credit ✓ |
|---|---|---|---|
| Sales | 8,800 | | ✓ |

(iii)

| Account name | Amount £ | Debit ✓ | Credit ✓ |
|---|---|---|---|
| Suspense | 720 | ✓ | |

## 39 JOHNNY JOINER

(a)

| Account name | Amount £ | Debit ✓ | Credit ✓ |
|---|---|---|---|
| Suspense | 14,363 | | ✓ |

(b)

| Account name | Amount £ | Debit ✓ | Credit ✓ |
|---|---|---|---|
| Suspense | 14,363 | ✓ | |
| Sales | 14,363 | | ✓ |

## 40    BUCKLEY DRAINS

**(a)**

| Account name | Amount £ | Debit ✓ | Credit ✓ |
|---|---|---|---|
| Suspense | 10,805 | | ✓ |

**(b)**

| Account name | Amount £ | Debit ✓ | Credit ✓ |
|---|---|---|---|
| Suspense | 10,805 | ✓ | |
| Purchase ledger control | 10,805 | | ✓ |

**(c)**    Show one reason for maintaining the journal

| | ✓ |
|---|---|
| To correct errors only | |
| To correct errors and record transactions that have not been recorded in any other book of prime entry | ✓ |
| To record transactions from every other book of prime entry. | |

## 41    MENDONCA

**(a)**

| Account name | Amount £ | Debit ✓ | Credit ✓ |
|---|---|---|---|
| Suspense | 1,980 | | ✓ |

**(b)**

| Account name | Amount £ | Debit ✓ | Credit ✓ |
|---|---|---|---|
| Suspense | 1,980 | ✓ | |
| Wages | 900 | ✓ | |
| Bank | 2,880 | | ✓ |

## 42    BEASANT

**(a)**

| Account name | Amount £ | Debit ✓ | Credit ✓ |
|---|---|---|---|
| Suspense | 15,000 | | ✓ |

**(b)**

| Account name | Amount £ | Debit ✓ | Credit ✓ |
|---|---|---|---|
| Suspense | 15,000 | ✓ | |
| Sales | 12,500 | | ✓ |
| VAT | 2,500 | | ✓ |

(c)    Show one reason for maintaining the journal

|  |  ✓ |
| --- | --- |
| To detect fraud |  |
| To record non-regular transactions | ✓ |
| To record goods sold on credit |  |

# POSTING JOURNAL ENTRIES TO LEDGER ACCOUNTS

## 43    PAT'S CAFE

(a)    What entry would be made in the suspense account to balance the trial balance?

| Account name | Amount £ | Debit ✓ | Credit ✓ |
| --- | --- | --- | --- |
| Suspense | 4,650 | ✓ |  |

(b)

| Account name | Balance £ | Debit ✓ | Credit ✓ |
| --- | --- | --- | --- |
| Bank interest paid | 235 | ✓ |  |
| Bank interest received | 61 |  | ✓ |
| Insurance | 550 | ✓ |  |
| Motor vehicles | 6500 | ✓ |  |

## 44    TWINKLE'S TRINKETS

(a)

| Account name | Amount £ | Debit ✓ | Credit ✓ |
| --- | --- | --- | --- |
| Suspense | 776 |  | ✓ |

(b)

| Account name | Balance £ | Debit ✓ | Credit ✓ |
| --- | --- | --- | --- |
| Motor expenses | 8,744 | ✓ |  |
| Repairs and renewals | 1,210 | ✓ |  |
| Rent payable | 3,700 | ✓ |  |
| Rent received | 1,700 |  | ✓ |

**45 SPARKS AND MENCER**

| Account name | Balance £ | Debit ✓ | Credit ✓ |
|---|---|---|---|
| Heat and light | 655 | ✓ | |
| Rates | 1,416 | ✓ | |
| Loan interest expense | 165 | ✓ | |
| Rent received | 119 | | ✓ |

# RE-DRAFT THE TRIAL BALANCE

**46 RICK'S RACERS**

| | | Balances at 1 July | |
|---|---|---|---|
| | | Debit | Credit £ |
| Motor vehicles | 24,200 | ✓ | |
| Plant and equipment | 22,350 | ✓ | |
| Inventory | 9,000 | ✓ | |
| Cash at bank | 11,217 | ✓ | |
| Cash | 150 | ✓ | |
| Sales ledger control | 131,275 | ✓ | |
| Purchases ledger control | 75,336 | | ✓ |
| VAT owing to HM Revenue and Customs | 15,127 | | ✓ |
| Capital | 26,247 | | ✓ |
| Bank loan | 12,500 | | ✓ |
| Sales | 276,132 | | ✓ |
| Purchases | 152,476 | ✓ | |
| Wages | 35,465 | ✓ | |
| Motor expenses | 3,617 | ✓ | |
| Repairs and renewals | 2,103 | ✓ | |
| Rent and rates | 3,283 | ✓ | |
| Light and heat | 4,012 | ✓ | |
| Insurance | 4,874 | ✓ | |
| Sundry expenses | 1,320 | ✓ | |
| Suspense account (credit balance) | | | |

## 47 PERCY POTS

| | Balances at 1 July | |
|---|---|---|
| | Debit £ | Credit £ |
| Motor vehicles | 22,348 | |
| Fixtures and fittings | 9,234 | |
| Inventory | 4,800 | |
| Bank | | 2,661 |
| Petty cash | 100 | |
| Sales ledger control | 61,025 | |
| Purchases ledger control | | 35,275 |
| VAT owing to HM Revenue and Customs | | 4,630 |
| Capital | | 4,852 |
| Sales | | 142,378 |
| Sales returns | 1,870 | |
| Purchases | 69,276 | |
| Wages | 13,500 | |
| Motor expenses | 873 | |
| Office expenses | 1,796 | |
| Rent and rates | 1,276 | |
| Heat and light | 1,022 | |
| Insurance | 1,629 | |
| Miscellaneous expenses | 1,047 | |
| Suspense account | | |
| **Total** | **189,796** | **189,796** |

**48    IVOR ISLAND**

| | Balances extracted on 30 April | Balances at 1 May | |
|---|---|---|---|
| | | Debit £ | Credit £ |
| Motor vehicles | 8,454 | 8,454 | |
| Office building | 28,676 | 28,676 | |
| Inventory | 15,369 | 15,369 | |
| Bank | 26,984 | 26,984 | |
| Petty cash | 459 | 459 | |
| Sales ledger control | 35,987 | 35,987 | |
| Purchases ledger control | 26,942 | | 26,942 |
| VAT (owing to HM Revenue and Customs) | 231 | | (W1) 941 |
| Capital | 98,106 | | 98,106 |
| Sales | 96,325 | | 96,325 |
| Purchase returns | 3,654 | | (W2) 3,954 |
| Purchases | 68,975 | 68,975 | |
| Wages | 18,564 | 18,564 | |
| Motor expenses | 1,269 | 1,269 | |
| Office expenses | 5,798 | 5,798 | |
| Rates | 4,300 | 4,300 | |
| Heat and light | 5,423 | 5,423 | |
| Insurance | 3,365 | 3,365 | |
| Misc. expenses | 2,645 | 2,645 | |
| Suspense account (credit balance) | 1,472 | nil | nil |
| **Totals** | | **226,268** | **226,268** |

**Workings:**

**(W1)**

**VAT**

| Details | Amount £ | Details | Amount £ |
|---|---|---|---|
| Balance b/f | 231 | Suspense | 586 |
| | | Suspense | 586 |
| Balance c/d | 941 | | |
| | **1,172** | | **1,172** |
| | | Balance b/d | 941 |

**(W2)**

**Purchase returns**

| Details | Amount £ | Details | Amount £ |
|---|---|---|---|
| Suspense | 2,256 | Balance b/d | 3,654 |
| | | Suspense | 2,556 |
| Balance c/d | 3,954 | | |
| | **6,210** | | **6,210** |
| | | Balance b/d | 3,954 |

## 49  RING OF ROSES

| | Balances at 1 July | |
|---|---|---|
| | Debit £ | Credit £ |
| Motor vehicles | 27,625 | |
| Plant and equipment | 5,000 | |
| Inventory | 7,350 | |
| Cash at bank | 14,345 | |
| Cash | 200 | |
| Sales ledger control | 121,275 | |
| Purchases ledger control | | 67,323 |
| VAT owing to HM Revenue and Customs | | 10,098 |
| Capital | | 22,291 |
| Sales | | 253,727 |
| Sales returns | 2,123 | |
| Purchases | 134,931 | |
| Purchase returns | | 9,872 |
| Wages | 34,250 | |
| Motor expenses | 1,797 | |
| Office expenses | 4,946 | |
| Rent and rates | 2,321 | |
| Heat and light | 3,123 | |
| Insurance | 4,025 | |
| Suspense account | | |
| **Total** | **363,311** | **363,311** |

## 50   HEARN

**Journal entries**

| Account name | Debit £ | Credit £ |
|---|---|---|
| Rent | 90 | |
| Suspense | | 90 |
| VAT | 120 | |
| Suspense | | 120 |

| | Balances extracted on 30 June £ | Balances at 1 July Debit £ | Balances at 1 July Credit £ |
|---|---|---|---|
| Sales ledger control | 34,560 | 34,560 | |
| Purchases ledger control | 21,420 | | 21,420 |
| VAT owing to HM Revenue and Customs | 3,412 | | 3,292 |
| Capital | 50,000 | | 50,000 |
| Sales | 201,327 | | 201,327 |
| Sales returns | 1,465 | 1,465 | |
| Purchases | 87,521 | 87,521 | |
| Purchase returns | 252 | | 252 |
| Plant and equipment | 15,200 | 15,200 | |
| Motor expenses | 4,310 | 4,310 | |
| Office expenses | 10,321 | 10,321 | |
| Rent and rates | 21,420 | 21,510 | |
| Heat and light | 8,920 | 8,920 | |
| Wages | 53,205 | 53,205 | |
| Irrecoverable debt | 1,450 | 1,450 | |
| Office equipment | 42,030 | 42,030 | |
| Bank overdraft | 4201 | | 4201 |
| Suspense account (debit balance) | 210 | | |
| **Totals** | | **280,492** | **280,492** |

## 51    RODMAN

**Journal entries**

| Account name | Debit £ | Credit £ |
|---|---|---|
| Suspense | 1,250 | |
| VAT | | 1,250 |
| Wages | 8,600 | |
| Suspense | | 8,600 |

| | Balances extracted on 30 June £ | Balances at 1 July | |
|---|---|---|---|
| | | Debit £ | Credit £ |
| Sales ledger control | 38,070 | 38,070 | |
| Purchases ledger control | 20,310 | | 20,310 |
| VAT owed from HM Revenue and Customs | 2,510 | 1,260 | |
| Capital | 70,000 | | 70,000 |
| Sales | 153,488 | | 153,488 |
| Sales returns | 2,135 | 2,135 | |
| Purchases | 63,261 | 63,261 | |
| Purchase returns | 542 | | 542 |
| Plant and equipment | 17,319 | 17,319 | |
| Motor expenses | 3,214 | 3,214 | |
| Office expenses | 6,421 | 6,421 | |
| Rent and rates | 17,414 | 17,414 | |
| Heat and light | 6,421 | 6,421 | |
| Wages | 45,532 | 54,132 | |
| Irrecoverable debt | 1,532 | 1,532 | |
| Office equipment | 35,313 | 35,313 | |
| Bank overdraft | 2,152 | | 2,152 |
| Suspense account (debit balance) | 7,350 | | |
| **Totals** | | **246,492** | **246,492** |

# UPDATE THE CASH BOOK

### 52   RIVERS LTD

(a) – (c)

| Date 20XX | Details | Bank £ | Date 20XX | Cheque number | Details | Bank £ |
|---|---|---|---|---|---|---|
| 01 June | Balance b/d | 3,115 | 01 June | 111013 | Indigo Beds | 650 |
| 17 June | Bracken Ltd | 300 | 01 June | 111014 | DirectFit | 1,420 |
| 21 June | Airfleet Interiors | 560 | 01 June | 111015 | Langdon | 60 |
| 22 June | Harris Homes | 333 | 01 June | 111016 | QPF Ltd | 615 |
| 12 June | Ayreshire Build | 970 | 02 June | 111017 | OMD Ltd | 815 |
| 23 June | Bank interest | 15 | 02 June | 111018 | Hamden Ltd | 450 |
| | | | 13 June | 111019 | Freeman & Cope | 522 |
| | | | 13 June | | Collins | 175 |
| | | | 20 June | | Rent | 500 |
| | | | 23 June | | Bank charges | 20 |
| | | | 23 June | | Balance c/d | 66 |
| | | 5,293 | | | | 5,293 |
| 24 June | Balance b/d | 66 | | | | |

### 53   LUXURY BATHROOMS

(a) – (c)

| Date | Details | Bank | Date | Cheque | Details | Bank |
|---|---|---|---|---|---|---|
| 01 April | Balance b/d | 17,845 | 01 April | 120045 | R Sterling Ltd | 8,850 |
| 19 April | Olsen & Lane | 2,150 | 01 April | 120046 | Bert Cooper | 2,250 |
| 22 April | Frith Ltd | 685 | 01 April | 120047 | Hetko & Sons | 64 |
| 22 April | Hodgetts & Co | 282 | 02 April | 120048 | Barrett Ltd | 3,256 |
| 04 April | Ricketts & Co | 465 | 02 April | 120049 | K Plomer | 542 |
| | | | 08 April | 120050 | I&E Brown | 655 |
| | | | 08 April | 120051 | T Roberts | 1,698 |
| | | | 14 April | | AMB Ltd | 2,265 |
| | | | 14 April | | D Draper | 2,950 |
| | | | 22 April | | Bank charges | 63 |
| | | | 23 April | | Overdraft fee | 25 |
| 24 April | Balance c/d | 1,191 | | | | |
| | | 22,618 | | | | 22,618 |
| | | | 25 April | | Balance b/d | 1,191 |

## 54    WHOLESALE FLOORING

### (a) – (c)

| Date 20XX | Details | Bank £ | Date 20XX | Cheque number | Details | Bank £ |
|---|---|---|---|---|---|---|
| | | | 01 June | | Balance b/d | 5,125 |
| 16 June | Beeston's | 550 | 01 June | 104373 | Good Iron | 890 |
| 19 June | Airfleet Exteriors | 3,025 | 01 June | 104374 | Ashworth and Co | 1,725 |
| 22 June | Jones's | 2,775 | 01 June | 104375 | Ironfit | 210 |
| 12 June | Aintree and Co | 1,250 | 05 June | 104376 | OSS Ltd | 1,275 |
| | | | 07 June | 104377 | Perfect Tools | 725 |
| | | | 08 June | 104378 | Campden Ltd | 784 |
| | | | 14 June | 104379 | Thornley and Thwaite | 675 |
| | | | 14 June | 104380 | Castle and Cove | 178 |
| | | | 20 June | | MD County Council | 400 |
| | | | 23 June | | Bank charges | 160 |
| 23 June | Balance c/d | 4,637 | 23 June | | Overdraft fee | 90 |
| | | 12,237 | | | | 12,237 |
| | | | 24 June | | Balance b/d | 4,637 |

## 55    24 HOUR TAXIS

### (a) – (c)

| Date 20XX | Details | Bank £ | Date 20XX | Cheque number | Details | Bank £ |
|---|---|---|---|---|---|---|
| 01 June | Balance b/d | 6,025 | 01 June | 102597 | Best Ideas | 910 |
| 18 June | Earnshaw's | 1,000 | 02 June | 102598 | Bentley and Burn | 2,010 |
| 19 June | Mainstreet Ltd | 1,206 | 02 June | 102599 | Bits and Bats | 315 |
| 21 June | Housley Inc | 1,725 | 03 June | 102600 | LPF Ltd | 1,725 |
| 12 June | Barron Homes | 1,475 | 07 June | 102601 | Essentials | 686 |
| | | | 08 June | 102602 | Hopburn Ltd | 675 |
| | | | 15 June | 102603 | Thistle Tools | 410 |
| | | | 15 June | 102604 | C Campbell Ltd | 275 |
| | | | 20 June | | AB Insurance | 1,250 |
| | | | 23 June | | Bank charges | 50 |
| | | | 23 June | | Overdraft fee | 25 |
| | | | 23 June | | Balance c/d | 3,100 |
| | | 11,431 | | | | 11,431 |
| 24 June | Balance b/d | 3,100 | | | | |

## 56   WOOD

### (a) – (c)

| Date 20XX | Details | Bank £ | Date 20XX | Cheque number | Details | Bank £ |
|---|---|---|---|---|---|---|
| 01 June | Balance b/d | 17,640 | | | | |
| 03 June | Bradley | 1,320 | 04 June | 110341 | Carr | 1,540 |
| 03 June | Cash sales | 9,420 | 04 June | 110342 | Ramsden | 980 |
| 03 June | Thanoj | 2,450 | 04 June | 110343 | Coulson | 750 |
| 21 June | Cash sales | 7,430 | 04 June | 110344 | Brodie | 570 |
| 21 June | Devitt | 1,990 | 04 June | 110345 | Jones | 550 |
| 17 June | Interest earned | 80 | 04 June | 110346 | Gritton | 740 |
| | | | 20 June | | Bore | 250 |
| | | | 12 June | | Southwell | 820 |
| | | | 20 June | | Direct Debit Blundell | 400 |
| | | | 23 June | | Balance c/d | 33,730 |
| | | **40,330** | | | | **40,330** |
| 24 June | Balance b/d | 33,730 | | | | |

## 57   PEARSON

### (a) – (c)

| Date 20XX | Details | Bank £ | Date 20XX | Cheque number | Details | Bank £ |
|---|---|---|---|---|---|---|
| 01 June | Balance b/d | 550 | 07 June | 110123 | Connell | 430 |
| 09 June | Cash sales | 840 | 07 June | 110124 | Renner | 720 |
| 14 June | Cash sales | 1,540 | 07 June | 110125 | Bond | 750 |
| 22 June | Cunnington | 1,730 | 07 June | 110126 | Hatton | 75 |
| 02 June | Interest received | 5 | 07 June | 110127 | Bull | 270 |
| | | | 07 June | 110128 | Black | 135 |
| | | | 07 June | 110129 | Southall | 740 |
| | | | 02 June | | McMenemy | 1,200 |
| | | | 20 June | | Findus | 300 |
| | | | 23 June | | Bank charges | 25 |
| | | | 23 June | | Balance c/d | 20 |
| | | **4,665** | | | | **4,665** |
| 24 June | Balance b/d | 20 | | | | |

**58    MCKEOWN**

**(a) – (c)**

| Date 20XX | Details | Bank £ | Date 20XX | Cheque number | Details | Bank £ |
|---|---|---|---|---|---|---|
| 01 June | Balance b/d | 7,180 | 07 June | 110157 | Williams | 430 |
| 12 June | Sherwood | 640 | 07 June | 110158 | Forecast | 520 |
| 14 June | Cash sales | 1,200 | 07 June | 110159 | Beasant | 1,240 |
| 22 June | Tweedy | 860 | 07 June | 110160 | Davison | 1,420 |
| 23 June | Butterwood | 440 | 07 June | 110161 | Mildenhall | 750 |
| 01 June | Interest received | 85 | 23 June | | Wilmott | 300 |
| 20 June | Coyne | 1,630 | | | | |
| 23 June | Interest received | 35 | | | | |
| | | | 23 June | | Balance c/d | 7,410 |
| | | 12,070 | | | | 12,070 |
| 24 June | Balance b/d | 7,410 | | | | |

# BANK RECONCILIATIONS

**59    RIVERS BANK RECONCILIATION**

| Balance per bank statement | £510 |
|---|---|
| **Add:** | |
| Name: Airfleet Interiors | £560 |
| Name: Harris Homes | £333 |
| **Total to add** | **£893** |
| **Less:** | |
| Name: OMD Ltd | £815 |
| Name: Freeman & Cope | £522 |
| **Total to subtract** | **£1,337** |
| **Balance as per cash book** | **£66** |

**60    LUXURY BATHROOMS BANK RECONCILIATION**

| Balance per bank statement | £82 |
|---|---|
| Add: | |
| Name: Frith Ltd | £685 |
| Name: Hodgetts & Co | £282 |
| Total to add | £967 |
| Less: | |
| Name: K Plomer | £542 |
| Name: T Roberts | £1,698 |
| Total to subtract | £2,240 |
| Balance as per cash book | (£1,191) |

**61    WHOLESALE FLOORING BANK RECONCILIATION**

| Balance per bank statement | (£9,584) |
|---|---|
| Add: | |
| Name: Airfleet Exteriors | £3,025 |
| Name: Jones's | £2,775 |
| Total to add | £5,800 |
| Less: | |
| Name: Thornley & Thwaite | £675 |
| Name: Castle & Cove | £178 |
| Total to subtract | £853 |
| Balance as per cash book | (£4,637) |

**62    24 HOUR TAXIS BANK RECONCILIATION**

| Balance per bank statement | £854 |
|---|---|
| Add: | |
| Name: Mainstreet Ltd | £1,206 |
| Name: Housley Inc | £1,725 |
| Total to add | £2,931 |
| Less: | |
| Name: Thistle Tools | £410 |
| Name: C Campbell Ltd | £275 |
| Total to subtract | £685 |
| Balance as per cash book | £3,100 |

## 63    WOOD BANK RECONCILIATION

(a)

| Balance per bank statement | £25,840 |
|---|---|
| Add: | |
| Name: Cash sales | £7,430 |
| Name: Devitt | £1,990 |
| Total to add | £9,420 |
| Less: | |
| Name: Ramsden | £980 |
| Name: Jones | £550 |
| Total to subtract | £1,530 |
| Balance as per cash book | £33,730 |

(b)

| Balance carried down<br>£ | Bank column totals<br>£ |
|---|---|
| 33,730 | 40,330 |

**Working:**

**Cash book**

| Date 20XX | Details | Bank £ | Date 20XX | Cheque number | Details | Bank £ |
|---|---|---|---|---|---|---|
| 01 June | Balance b/d | 17,640 | | | | |
| 03 June | Bradley | 1,320 | 04 June | 110341 | Carr | 1,540 |
| 03 June | Cash sales | 9,420 | 04 June | 110342 | Ramsden | 980 |
| 03 June | Thanoj | 2,450 | 04 June | 110343 | Coulson | 750 |
| 21 June | Cash sales | 7,430 | 04 June | 110344 | Brodie | 570 |
| 21 June | Devitt | 1,990 | 04 June | 110345 | Jones | 550 |
| 17 June | Interest earned | 80 | 04 June | 110346 | Gritton | 740 |
| | | | 20 June | | Bore | 250 |
| | | | 12 June | | Southwell | 820 |
| | | | 20 June | | Direct Debit Blundell | 400 |
| | | | 23 June | | Balance c/d | 33,730 |
| | | 40,330 | | | | 40,330 |
| 24 June | Balance b/d | 33,730 | | | | |

## 64 PEARSON BANK RECONCILIATION

(a)

| Balance per bank statement | (£105) |
|---|---|
| Add: | |
| Name: Cunnington | £1,730 |
| Total to add | £1,730 |
| Less: | |
| Name: Renner | £720 |
| Name: Bond | £750 |
| Name: Black | £135 |
| Total to subtract | £1,605 |
| Balance as per cash book | £20 |

(b) **Show which security procedure listed below Pearson should use to ensure the security of receipts from customers.**

| | ✓ |
|---|---|
| Cash received from customers should be kept in a locked safe until banked | ✓ |
| Cash should be banked on a monthly basis | |
| Cheques received too late to bank should be posted through the bank's letter box | |

## 65 MCKEOWN BANK RECONCILIATION

(a)

| Balance per bank statement | £8,770 |
|---|---|
| Add: | |
| Name: Tweedy | £860 |
| Name: Butterwood | £440 |
| Total to add | £1,300 |
| Less: | |
| Name: Beasant | £1,240 |
| Name: Davison | £1,420 |
| Total to subtract | £2,660 |
| Balance as per cash book | £7,410 |

(b)

| Balance carried down | Bank column totals |
|---|---|
| £ | £ |
| 7,410 | 12,070 |

**Workings:**

**Cash book**

| Date 20XX | Details | Bank £ | Date 20XX | Cheque number | Details | Bank £ |
|---|---|---|---|---|---|---|
| 01 June | Balance b/d | 7,180 | 07 June | 110157 | Williams | 430 |
| 12 June | Sherwood | 640 | 07 June | 110158 | Forecast | 520 |
| 14 June | Cash sales | 1,200 | 07 June | 110159 | Beasant | 1,240 |
| 22 June | Tweedy | 860 | 07 June | 110160 | Davison | 1,420 |
| 23 June | Butterwood | 440 | 07 June | 110161 | Mildenhall | 750 |
| 01 June | Interest received | 85 | 23 June | | Wilmott | 300 |
| 20 June | Coyne | 1,630 | | | | |
| 23 June | Interest received | 35 | | | | |
| | | | 23 June | | Balance c/d | 7,410 |
| | | 12,070 | | | | 12,070 |
| 24 June | Balance b/d | 7,410 | | | | |

# PREPARE AND RECONCILE SALES/PURCHASE LEDGER CONTROL ACCOUNTS

## 66 MONSTER MUNCHIES

(a)

| Details | Amount £ | Debit ✓ | Credit ✓ |
|---|---|---|---|
| Balance of receivables at 1 June | 48,000 | ✓ | |
| Goods sold on credit | 12,415 | ✓ | |
| Receipts from credit customers | 22,513 | | ✓ |
| Discount allowed | 465 | | ✓ |
| Sales returns from credit customers | 320 | | ✓ |

(b)

| Dr £37,117 | ✓ |
|---|---|

(c)

| | £ |
|---|---|
| Sales ledger control account balance as at 30 June | 37,117 |
| Total of subsidiary (sales) ledger accounts as at 30 June | 36,797 |
| Difference | 320 |

**(d)**

| | |
|---|---|
| Sales returns may have been omitted from the subsidiary ledger. | |
| Discounts allowed may have been omitted from the subsidiary ledger. | |
| Sales returns may have been entered in the subsidiary ledger twice. | ✓ |
| Discounts allowed may have been entered in the subsidiary ledger twice. | ✓ |

**(e)**

| | |
|---|---|
| Reconciliation of the sales ledger control account assures managers that the amount showing as owed to suppliers is correct. | |
| Reconciliation of the sales ledger control account assures managers that the amount showing as outstanding from customers is correct. | ✓ |
| Reconciliation of the sales ledger control account will show if a purchase invoice has been omitted from the purchase ledger. | |
| Reconciliation of the sales ledger control account will show if a purchase invoice has been omitted from the sales ledger. | |

**67   JACK'S BOX**

**(a)**

| Details | Amount £ | Debit ✓ | Credit ✓ |
|---|---|---|---|
| Balance of receivables at 1 April | 60,589 | ✓ | |
| Goods sold on credit | 26,869 | ✓ | |
| Payments received from credit customers | 29,411 | | ✓ |
| Discount allowed | 598 | | ✓ |
| Goods returned from credit customers | 1,223 | | ✓ |

**(b)**

| | |
|---|---|
| Dr £55,030 | |
| Cr £55,030 | |
| Dr £56,226 | ✓ |
| Cr £56,226 | |
| Dr £52,584 | |
| Cr £52,584 | |

**(c)**

|  | £ |
|---|---|
| Sales Ledger control account balances as at 30 April | 56,226 |
| Total of subsidiary (sales) ledger accounts as at 30 April | 55,003 |
| Difference | 1,223 |

**(d)**

|  | ✓ |
|---|---|
| Sales returns may have been omitted from the subsidiary ledger. |  |
| Discounts allowed may have been omitted from the subsidiary ledger. |  |
| Sales returns have been entered into the subsidiary ledger twice. | ✓ |
| Discounts allowed have been entered into subsidiary ledger twice. |  |

**(e)**

|  | ✓ |
|---|---|
| Reconciliation of the sales ledger control account will show if a purchase invoice has been omitted from the purchases ledger. |  |
| Reconciliation of the sales ledger control account will show if a sales invoice has been omitted from the purchases ledger. |  |
| Reconciliation of the sales ledger control account assures managers that the amount showing due to suppliers is correct. |  |
| Reconciliation of the sales ledger control account assures managers that the amount showing due from customers is correct. | ✓ |

## 68  CILLA'S SINKS

**(a)**

| Details | Amount £ | Debit ✓ | Credit ✓ |
|---|---|---|---|
| Balance of payables at 1 June | 52,150 |  | ✓ |
| Goods bought on credit | 19,215 |  | ✓ |
| Payments made to credit suppliers | 19,073 | ✓ |  |
| Discount received | 284 | ✓ |  |
| Goods returned to credit suppliers | 1,023 | ✓ |  |

**(b)**

| Cr £50,985 | ✓ |
|---|---|

**(c)**

|  | £ |
|---|---|
| Purchase ledger control account balance as at 30 June | 50,985 |
| Total of subsidiary (purchase) ledger accounts as at 30 June | 52,008 |
| Difference | 1,023 |

**(d)**

| | |
|---|---|
| Goods returned may have been omitted from the subsidiary ledger. | ✓ |
| Discounts received may have been omitted from the subsidiary ledger. | |
| Goods returned may have been entered in the subsidiary ledger twice. | |
| Discounts received may have been entered into the subsidiary ledger twice. | |

**(e)**

| | |
|---|---|
| Reconciliation of the PLCA will help to identify any supplier invoices that have been omitted in error. | ✓ |
| Reconciliation of the purchase ledger control account will show if a sales invoice has been omitted from the purchase ledger. | |
| Reconciliation of the purchase ledger control account will show if a sales invoice has been omitted from the sales ledger. | |
| Reconciliation of the purchase ledger control account will help to identify any discounts allowed that have been omitted in error. | |

## 69 VIK'S TRICKS

**(a)**

| Details | Amount £ | Debit ✓ | Credit ✓ |
|---|---|---|---|
| Balance of receivables at 1 June | 58,120 | ✓ | |
| Goods sold on credit | 20,013 | ✓ | |
| Receipts from credit customers | 22,327 | | ✓ |
| Discount allowed | 501 | | ✓ |
| Sales returns from credit customers | 970 | | ✓ |

**(b)**

| Dr £54,335 | ✓ |
|---|---|

**(c)**

| | £ |
|---|---|
| Sales ledger control account balance as at 30 June | 54,335 |
| Total of subsidiary (sales) ledger accounts as at 30 June | 55,305 |
| Difference | 970 |

**(d)**

| | |
|---|---|
| Discounts allowed may have been entered in the subsidiary ledger twice. | |
| Discounts allowed may have been omitted from the subsidiary ledger. | ✓ |
| Sales returns may have been entered in the subsidiary ledger twice. | |
| Sales returns may have been omitted from the subsidiary ledger. | ✓ |

**(e)**

| | |
|---|---|
| Reconciliation of the sales ledger control account will help to identify any customer invoices that have been omitted in error. | ✓ |
| Reconciliation of the sales ledger control account will show if a purchase invoice has been omitted from the sales ledger. | |
| Reconciliation of the sales ledger control account will show if a purchase invoice has been omitted from the purchase ledger. | |
| Reconciliation of the sales ledger control account will help to identify any discounts received that have been omitted in error. | |

## 70 ZHANG

**(a)**

**SLCA**

| Details | Amount £ | Details | Amount £ |
|---|---|---|---|
| Balance b/d | 65,830 | SBD overcast | 1,200 |
| | | Discount given | 210 |
| | | Balance c/d | 64,420 |
| | **65,830** | | **65,830** |
| Balance b/d | 64,420 | | |

**List of balances:**

|  | £ |
|---|---|
| Total: | 65,090 |
| Contra missing | (800) |
| Credit note posted twice | 130 |
| Revised total: | 64,420 |

**(b)** **Show whether the following statements are true or false:**

|  | True ✓ | False ✓ |
|---|---|---|
| An aged trade receivables analysis is used when chasing customers for outstanding payments. | ✓ |  |
| An aged trade receivables analysis is sent to credit customers when payments are being requested. |  | ✓ |

## 71 HANDYSIDE

**(a)**

**PLCA**

| Details | Amount £ | Details | Amount £ |
|---|---|---|---|
| Returns | 120 | Balance b/d | 25,360 |
|  |  | Missing invoice | 720 |
| Balance c/d | 25,960 |  |  |
|  | **26,080** |  | **26,080** |
|  |  | Balance b/d | 25,960 |

**List of balances:**

|  | £ |
|---|---|
| Total | 26,000 |
| Net amount entered | 400 |
| Returns | (350) |
| Transposition error | (90) |
| Revised total | 25,960 |

**(b)** **Show whether the following statements are true or false:**

|  | True ✓ | False ✓ |
|---|---|---|
| The purchases ledger control account enables a business to see how much is owed to individual suppliers |  | ✓ |
| The purchases ledger control account total should reconcile to the total of the list of supplier balances in the purchases ledger | ✓ |  |

# VAT CONTROL ACCOUNT

## 72 RING RING TELEPHONE

**(a)**

### VAT control

| Details | Amount £ | Details | Amount £ |
|---|---|---|---|
| Sales returns | 360 | Sales | 30,600 |
| Purchases | 16,200 | Cash sales | 48 |
| | | Purchases returns | 1,160 |
| Balance c/d | 15,248 | | |
| | **31,808** | | **31,808** |
| | | Balance b/d | 15,248 |

**(b)** No – it is £15,248 owed **to** HMRC

**(c)**

| | £ | Debit | Credit |
|---|---|---|---|
| Balance brought down | 38,900 | ✓ | |

**Workings:**

### VAT control

| Details | Amount £ | Details | Amount £ |
|---|---|---|---|
| Debit balances | 93,800 | Credit balances | 54,400 |
| Purchase of equipment | 400 | Cash sales | 900 |
| | | | |
| | | Balance c/d | 38,900 |
| | **94,200** | | **94,200** |
| Balance b/d | 38,900 | | |

## 73 JO'S JOINERS

**(a)**

### VAT Control

| Details | Amount £ | Details | Amount £ |
|---|---|---|---|
| Purchases | 21,000 | Sales | 31,200 |
| Sales returns | 720 | Cash sales | 120 |
| | | Purchases returns | 1,088 |
| | | | |
| Balance c/d | 10,688 | | |
| | **32,408** | | **32,408** |
| | | Balance b/d | 10,688 |

**(b)** Yes

**74  PHILIP'S CABINS**

**(a)**

**VAT control**

| Details | Amount £ | Details | Amount £ |
|---|---|---|---|
| Sales returns | 600 | Sales | 35,960 |
| Purchases | 20,040 | Cash sales | 112 |
| | | Purchases returns | 1,144 |
| Balance c/d | 16,576 | | |
| | **37,216** | | **37,216** |
| | | Balance b/d | 16,576 |

**(b)**  No – the amount owed to HMRC is £16,576.

**75  DISLEY**

**(a)**

| | £ | Debit | Credit |
|---|---|---|---|
| VAT total in the sales day book | 65,420 | | 65,420 |
| VAT total in the purchases day book | 21,340 | 21,340 | |
| VAT total in the sales returns day book | 480 | 480 | |
| VAT balance brought forward, owed to HMRC | 24,910 | | 24,910 |
| VAT on irrecoverable debts | 830 | 830 | |
| VAT on petty cash expenses paid | 210 | 210 | |

**(b)**  No – the amount owed to HMRC is £67,470.

**(c)**

| | £ | Debit | Credit |
|---|---|---|---|
| Balance brought down | 19,730 | | ✓ |

**Workings:**

**VAT control**

| Details | Amount £ | Details | Amount £ |
|---|---|---|---|
| Debit balances | 42,300 | Credit balances | 61,250 |
| Irrecoverable debt | 200 | Discounts received | 980 |
| | | | |
| Balance c/d | 19,730 | | |
| | **62,230** | | **62,230** |
| | | Balance b/d | 19,730 |

## 76   KERR

(a)   **Show whether each item is a debit or credit balance by copying the amount into the correct column**

| | £ | Debit | Credit |
|---|---|---|---|
| VAT total in the purchase returns day book | 1,320 | | 1,320 |
| VAT total in discounts received day book | 400 | | 400 |
| VAT on cash purchases | 2,670 | 2,670 | |
| VAT on the sale of equipment | 970 | | 970 |
| VAT total in discounts allowed day book | 500 | 500 | |
| VAT refund received from HMRC | 2,580 | | 2,580 |
| VAT on cash sales | 5,880 | | 5,880 |
| VAT balance brought forward, due from HMRC | 2,580 | 2,580 | |

(b)   Yes – the amount owed is correct

## 77   NEILSON

(a)

| | £ | Debit | Credit |
|---|---|---|---|
| VAT total in the sales day book | 54,670 | | 54,670 |
| VAT total in the purchases day book | 26,340 | 26,340 | |
| VAT total in the sales returns day book | 1,240 | 1,240 | |
| VAT total in the purchases returns day book | 760 | | 760 |
| VAT on sale of equipment | 3,210 | | 3,210 |
| VAT on petty cash expenses paid | 500 | 500 | |
| VAT balance brought forward, owed to HMRC | 42,180 | | 42,180 |
| VAT on irrecoverable debts | 430 | 430 | |
| VAT paid to HMRC during the period | 32,150 | 32,150 | |
| VAT on cash sales | 6,540 | | 6,540 |
| VAT on cash purchases | 7,520 | 7,520 | |
| VAT total in discounts allowed day book | 1,130 | 1,130 | |
| VAT total in discounts received day book | 980 | | 980 |

(b)   Yes – the amount owed is correct

# THE BANKING SYSTEM

**78  BLOSSOM BLOOMS**

(a)

| Checks to be made | Cheque | Telephone credit card payment |
|---|:---:|:---:|
| Check expiry date | ✓ | |
| Check issue number | ✓ | ✓ |
| Check not post dated | | ✓ |
| Check security number | ✓ | |
| Check words and figures match | | ✓ |
| Check card has not been tampered with | ✓ | ✓ |

(b)   When Blossom Blooms makes payments to suppliers by debit card, the amount paid affects the bank current account

**True**

When Blossom Blooms makes payments to suppliers by credit card, the amount paid affects the bank current account

**False**

**79  PETE'S PARROTS**

(a)

| Checks to be made | Cheque ✓ | Telephone credit card payment ✓ |
|---|:---:|:---:|
| Check expiry date | | ✓ |
| Check issue number | | |
| Check not posted dated | ✓ | |
| Check security number | | ✓ |
| Check words and figures match | ✓ | |
| Check card has not been tampered with | | |

(b)   When Pete's Parrots makes payments to suppliers by credit card, the amount does not leave the bank current account immediately

**True**

When Pete's Parrots makes payments to suppliers by debit card, the amount paid affects the bank current account

**True**

## 80  BANK EFFECTS 1

**Which TWO balances will NOT reduce funds in the bank balance of the payer at the date of payment?**

|  |  |
|---|---|
| Standing order |  |
| Cheque payment | ✓ |
| CHAPS payment |  |
| Credit card payment | ✓ |

## 81  BANK EFFECTS 2

**Which THREE balances WILL reduce funds in the bank balance of the payer at the date of payment?**

|  |  |
|---|---|
| Direct debit | ✓ |
| Building society cheque payment |  |
| Debit card payment | ✓ |
| BACS payment | ✓ |

## 82  METHODS OF PAYMENT 1

Match the payment need with the most likely method of payment to be used.

| | |
|---|---|
| Replacement batteries for office clock | CHAPS payment |
| Payment to complete the purchase of a new building, which needs to clear today | Debit/Credit card |
| Fixed monthly charge for rent | Direct debit |
| Payment for telephone bill, which fluctuates monthly | Cheque |
| Payment to regular supplier | Petty cash |
| Online purchase of computer equipment | Standing order |

## 83   METHODS OF PAYMENT 2

Match the payment with the description below

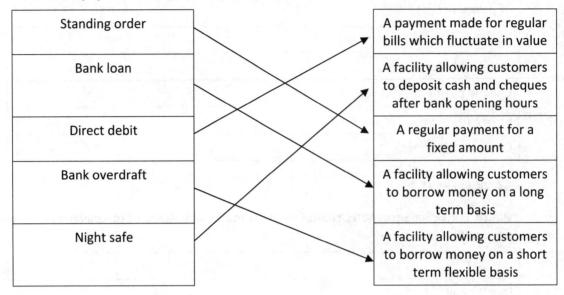

# Section 3

# MOCK ASSESSMENT QUESTIONS

**TASK 1**                                                       **(12 MARKS)**

**(a)**    **State whether the items below are true or false.**

|  | True ✓ | False ✓ |
|---|---|---|
| A direct debit is an instruction to a customer's bank to make regular payments, which are usually of a fixed amount. |  |  |
| A cheque which is 7 months past the date of the cheque is considered to be 'out of date'. |  |  |
| The drawer of a cheque is the account holder who is making the payment. |  |  |

**(b)**    **State whether the items below are true or false.**

|  | True ✓ | False ✓ |
|---|---|---|
| When Gates makes payments to suppliers by credit card the amount paid affects the bank current account. |  |  |
| When Gates makes payments to suppliers by debit card the amount paid affects the bank current account. |  |  |
| A cheque payment does not appear on the bank statement. |  |  |
| An unpresented cheque is a cheque payment that has cleared the bank prior to the reconciliation of the bank being performed. |  |  |

**(c)**    **Show which of the errors below are, or are not, disclosed by the trial balance.**

| Error in the general ledger | Error disclosed by the trial balance ✓ | Error NOT disclosed by the trial balance ✓ |
|---|---|---|
| Recording a bank payment for purchases on the debit side of both the bank and purchases account. |  |  |
| Recording a payment for rent and rates in a non-current assets account. |  |  |
| Recording a sales invoice in the sales account only. |  |  |
| Incorrectly calculating the balance brought down on the rent account. |  |  |

**(d)** **Show which error is an error of principle.**

| Error | ✓ |
|---|---|
| Recording a bank payment for office expenses on the debit side of the office furniture account. | |
| Recording a payment for motor expenses in the bank account, motor expenses account and miscellaneous expenses account. | |
| Recording a payment by cheque to a credit supplier in the bank account and purchases ledger control account only. | |
| Recording a cash payment for travel expenses in the cash account only. | |

## TASK 2 (12 MARKS)

Beesley pays its employees by cheque every month and maintains a wages control account. A summary of last month's payroll transactions is shown below:

| Item | £ |
|---|---|
| Gross wages | 26,500 |
| Employers' NI | 2,680 |
| Employees' NI | 2,760 |
| Income tax | 4,871 |
| Employer pension contributions | 1,000 |
| Employee pension contributions | 750 |

**Record the journal entries needed in the general ledger to:**

**(i)** **Record the wages expense**

**(ii)** **Record the HM Revenue and Customs liability**

**(iii)** **Record the net wages paid to the employees**

**(iv)** **Record the pension liability**

(i)

| Account name | Amount £ | Debit ✓ | Credit ✓ |
|---|---|---|---|
| | | | |
| | | | |

(ii)

| Account name | Amount £ | Debit ✓ | Credit ✓ |
|---|---|---|---|
| | | | |
| | | | |

(iii)

| Account name | Amount £ | Debit ✓ | Credit ✓ |
|---|---|---|---|
| | | | |
| | | | |

(iv)

| Account name | Amount £ | Debit ✓ | Credit ✓ |
|---|---|---|---|
| | | | |
| | | | |

Picklist for each: Bank, Employees NI, Employers NI, HM Revenue and Customs, Income tax, Net wages, Pension, Trade Union, Wages control, Wages expense.

## TASK 3                                                                (10 MARKS)

A credit customer, Halpert, has ceased trading owing Schrute £2,000 plus VAT at 20%

**(a)    Record the journal entries needed in the general ledger to write off Halpert's debt.**

| Account name | Amount £ | Debit ✓ | Credit ✓ |
|---|---|---|---|
| | | | |
| | | | |
| | | | |

Select your account names from the following list: Schrute, Irrecoverable debts, Halpert, Purchases, Purchases ledger control, Sales, Sales ledger control, VAT.

**(b)**    Scott has started a new business, Scarn, and a new set of accounts is to be opened. A partially completed journal to record a selection of the opening entries is shown below.

**Record the journal entries needed in the accounts in the general ledger of Scarn to deal with the opening entries.**

| Account name | Amount £ | Debit ✓ | Credit ✓ |
|---|---|---|---|
| Cash at bank | 7,250 | | |
| Bank loan | 5,000 | | |
| Capital | 10,000 | | |
| Motor vehicles | 5,400 | | |
| Commission received | 575 | | |
| Stationery | 300 | | |
| Sundry expenses | 225 | | |
| Advertising | 1,000 | | |
| Rent and rates | 1,400 | | |
| **Journal to record the opening entries of new business** | | | |

**TASK 4** (10 MARKS)

| | £ |
|---|---|
| VAT owing from HM Revenue and Customs at 1 June | 16,750 |
| VAT total in the purchases day book | 23,450 |
| VAT total in the sales day book | 46,750 |
| VAT total in the purchases returns day book | 230 |
| VAT total in the discounts allowed day book | 870 |
| VAT on cash sales | 3,450 |
| VAT on petty cash payments | 70 |
| VAT refund received from HM Revenue and Customs | 6,430 |
| VAT on irrecoverable debts written off | 640 |
| VAT on the sale of office equipment | 1,230 |

**Show how each of the transactions would be recorded in the VAT control account by entering items into the appropriate side of the control account, stating whether the balance is owed to HM Revenue and Customs or recoverable from HM Revenue and Customs.**

**VAT control**

| Details | Amount £ | Details | Amount £ |
|---|---|---|---|
| | | | |
| | | | |
| | | | |
| | | | |
| | | | |
| | | | |
| | | | |
| | | | |

Picklist: Balance b/d, Balance c/d, Sales, Purchases, Sales returns, Purchase returns, Cash sales, VAT refund, Irrecoverable debts, Office equipment sold, Discounts allowed, Petty cash

**TASK 5** (14 MARKS)

This is a summary of transactions with suppliers of Wuph during the month of May.

(a) **Show whether each entry will be a debit or credit in the purchases ledger control account in the general ledger.**

| Details | Amount £ | Debit ✓ | Credit ✓ |
|---|---|---|---|
| Balance of payables at 1 May | 89,726 | | |
| Credit purchases | 62,362 | | |
| Cheque payments to payables | 87,251 | | |
| Discounts received | 11,928 | | |
| Returns outwards | 12,987 | | |

(b) **What will be the balance brought down on 1 May on the above account?**

| | ✓ |
|---|---|
| Dr £ 49,804 | |
| Cr £ 49,804 | |
| Dr £ 39,922 | |
| Cr £ 39,922 | |
| Dr £ 65,896 | |
| Cr £ 65,896 | |

(c) The following credit balances were in the purchases ledger on 1 June.

| | £ |
|---|---|
| DMI | 8,336 |
| Ronnie's | 7,361 |
| Cynthia | 9,101 |
| Roy's Ltd | 9,872 |
| Goldenface | 4,321 |
| Levenson | 12,859 |

**Reconcile the balances shown above with the sales ledger control account balance you have calculated in part (a).**

| | £ |
|---|---|
| Purchase ledger control account balance as at 1 June | |
| Total of purchase ledger accounts as at 30 June | |
| Difference | |

**(d)    What may have caused the difference you calculated in part (c)?**

| | |
|---|---|
| Goods returned may have been entered in the purchases ledger twice from the purchases ledger. | |
| Discounts received may have been entered in the purchases ledger twice. | |
| Discounts received may have been omitted from the purchases ledger control account. | |
| Discounts received may have been omitted from the purchases ledger. | |

**(e)**    It is important to reconcile the purchases ledger control account on a regular basis.

**Which of the following statements is true?**

| | |
|---|---|
| Reconciliation of the purchases ledger control account assures managers that the amount showing as outstanding to customers is correct. | |
| Reconciliation of the purchases ledger control account assures managers that the amount showing as outstanding from suppliers is correct. | |
| Reconciliation of the purchases ledger control account assures managers that the amount showing as outstanding to suppliers is correct. | |
| Reconciliation of the purchases ledger control account will show if a purchase invoice has been omitted from the purchases ledger. | |

**TASK 6**                                                                                    **(10 MARKS)**

On 28 April Dunder Mifflin received the following bank statement as at 24 April.

| SKB Bank plc | | | | | |
|---|---|---|---|---|---|
| **68 London Road, Reading, RG8 4RN** | | | | | |
| To: Dunder Mifflin | Account No: 55548921 | | 24 April 20XX | | |
| **Statement of Account** | | | | | |
| **Date** | **Detail** | **Paid out** | **Paid in** | **Balance** | |
| **20XX** | | £ | £ | £ | |
| 03 April | Balance b/d | | | 18,000 | C |
| 03 April | Cheque 120045 | 6,234 | | 11,766 | C |
| 04 April | Bank Giro Prince Paper | | 342 | 12,108 | C |
| 04 April | Cheque 120046 | 1,632 | | 10,476 | C |
| 05 April | Cheque 120047 | 41 | | 10,435 | C |
| 08 April | Cheque 120048 | 4,444 | | 5,991 | C |
| 14 April | Direct debit Staples Ltd | 2,878 | | 3,113 | C |
| 14 April | Direct debit Steamtown Mall | 2,865 | | 248 | C |
| 14 April | Cheque 120050 | 432 | | 184 | D |
| 22 April | Paid in at SKB Bank | | 5,321 | 5,137 | C |
| 22 April | Bank charges | 54 | | 5,083 | C |
| 23 April | Overdraft fee | 27 | | 5,056 | C |
| D = Debit    C = Credit | | | | | |

The cash book as at 24 April is shown below.

**Cash Book**

| Date | Details | Bank | Date | Cheque | Details | Bank |
|---|---|---|---|---|---|---|
| 01 April | Balance b/d | 18,000 | 01 April | 120045 | Mose Ltd | 6,234 |
| 19 April | Wallace | 5,321 | 01 April | 120046 | Sabre | 1,632 |
| 22 April | Bennett | 685 | 01 April | 120047 | Hannan | 41 |
| 22 April | Lewis | 282 | 02 April | 120048 | Flinderson | 4,444 |
| | | | 02 April | 120049 | Bratton | 542 |
| | | | 08 April | 120050 | Flax | 432 |
| | | | 08 April | 120051 | Vickers | 1,698 |
| | | | 14 April | DD | Staples | 2,878 |
| | | | | | | |
| | | | | | | |
| | | | | | | |
| | | | | | | |
| | | | | | | |
| | | | | | | |

Details column options: Balance b/d, balance c/d, Bank charges, Mose Ltd, Sabre, Hannan, Steamtown Mall, Flinderson, Bratton, Flax, Vickers, Wallace, Bennett, Lewis, Prince Paper, Opening balance, Overdraft fees

(a)     **Check the items on the bank statement against the items in the cash book.**

(b)     **Enter any items in the cash book as needed.**

(c)     **Total the cash book and clearly show the balance carried down at 24 April (closing balance) and brought down at 25 April (opening balance).**

## TASK 7 (14 MARKS)

Martinez Ltd received the following bank statement for the month of June.

| | | | | |
|---|---|---|---|---|
| **Four Kings Bank PLC** | | | | |
| To: Martinez Ltd | | Account No: 16135844 | | 30 June 20XX |
| **Bank statement** | | | | |
| Date | Detail | Paid out | Paid in | Balance |
| 20XX | | £ | £ | £ |
| 04 June | Balance b/d | | | 6,025 C |
| 05 June | Cheque 102597 | 910 | | 5,115 C |
| 05 June | Cheque 102598 | 2,010 | | 3,105 C |
| 05 June | Cheque 102599 | 315 | | 2,790 C |
| 11 June | Cheque 102602 | 675 | | 2,115 C |
| 12 June | Bank Giro credit California | | 1,475 | 3,590 C |
| 13 June | Cheque 102600 | 1,725 | | 1,865 C |
| 15 June | Cheque 102601 | 686 | | 1,179 C |
| 19 June | Paid in at Four Kings Bank | | 1,000 | 2,179 C |
| 20 June | Direct debit AB Insurance | 1,250 | | 929 C |
| 23 June | Bank charges | 50 | | 879 C |
| 23 June | Overdraft fee | 25 | | 854 C |
| D = Debit   C = Credit | | | | |

Martinez Ltd's cash book is shown below:

| Date 20XX | Details | Bank £ | Date 20XX | Cheque number | Details | Bank £ |
|---|---|---|---|---|---|---|
| 01 June | Balance b/d | 6,025 | 01 June | 102597 | Cordray | 910 |
| 12 June | Robert California | 1,475 | 02 June | 102598 | Palmer | 2,010 |
| 18 June | Martin | 1,000 | 02 June | 102599 | Filippelli | 315 |
| 19 June | Packer Ltd | 1,206 | 03 June | 102600 | Anderson Ltd | 1,725 |
| 21 June | Miner Ltd | 1,725 | 07 June | 102601 | Brent | 686 |
| | | | 08 June | 102602 | Poor Richard's Ltd | 675 |
| | | | 15 June | 102603 | D'Angelo | 410 |
| | | | 15 June | 102604 | Klump | 275 |
| | | | 20 June | | Ping Ltd | 1,250 |
| | | | 23 June | | Bank charges | 50 |
| | | | 23 June | | Overdraft fee | 25 |

You are preparing to complete the bank reconciliation statement at 30 June, starting with the balance taken from the bank statement.

**(a)** Identify the details of TWO outstanding lodgements that should be entered into the bank reconciliation statement and show whether the amounts should be added or subtracted.

| Details | Amount £ | Add ✓ | Subtract ✓ |
|---|---|---|---|
| | | | |
| | | | |

Details options: Ping Ltd, D'Angelo, Klump, Brent, Poor Richard's Ltd, Anderson Ltd, Filippelli, Palmer, Cordray, Robert California, Miner Ltd, Packer Ltd, Martin.

**(b)** Identify the details of TWO unpresented cheques that should be entered into the bank reconciliation statement and show whether the amounts should be added or subtracted.

| Details | Amount £ | Add ✓ | Subtract ✓ |
|---|---|---|---|
| | | | |
| | | | |

Details options: Ping Ltd, D'Angelo, Klump, Brent, Poor Richard's Ltd, Anderson Ltd, Filippelli, Palmer, Cordray, Robert California, Miner Ltd, Packer Ltd, Martin.

**(c)** Complete the bank reconciliation statement for Martinez Ltd for 30 June.

**Bank reconciliation statement as at 30 June for Martinez Ltd.**

| Balance per bank statement | £ |
|---|---|
| **Outstanding lodgements** | |
| Name: | £ |
| Name: | £ |
| **Unpresented cheques** | |
| Name: | £ |
| Name: | £ |
| **Balance as per cash book** | £ |

**(d)** Check that the bank reconciliation statement in (c) has been completed correctly by calculating:

- The balance carried down in the cash book

- The total of each of the cash book columns after the balance carried down has been recorded.

| Balance carried down £ | Cash book column totals £ |
|---|---|
| | |

## TASK 8 (14 MARKS)

(a) Bernard's trial balance was extracted and did not balance. The debit column of the trial balance totalled £109,798 and the credit column totalled £219,666.

**What entry would be made in the suspense account to balance the trial balance?**

| Account name | Amount £ | Debit ✓ | Credit ✓ |
|---|---|---|---|
|  |  |  |  |
|  |  |  |  |

(b) Hudson's initial trial balance includes a suspense account with a balance of £8,640.

The error has been traced to the purchase day-book shown below.

**Purchase day-book**

| Date 20XX | Details | Invoice number | Total £ | VAT £ | Net £ |
|---|---|---|---|---|---|
| 30 Jun | Philbin | 2,763 | 2,400 | 400 | 2,000 |
| 30 Jun | Lappin | 2,764 | 3,120 | 520 | 2,600 |
| 30 Jun | Malone | 2,765 | 4,080 | 680 | 3,400 |
|  | **Totals** |  | 960 | 1,600 | 8,000 |

**Identify the error and record the journal entries needed in the general ledger to:**

**(i)    remove the incorrect entry**

**(ii)   record the correct entry**

**(iii)  remove the suspense account balance.**

(i)

| Account name | Amount £ | Debit ✓ | Credit ✓ |
|---|---|---|---|
|  |  |  |  |

(ii)

| Account name | Amount £ | Debit ✓ | Credit ✓ |
|---|---|---|---|
|  |  |  |  |

(iii)

| Account name | Amount £ | Debit ✓ | Credit ✓ |
|---|---|---|---|
|  |  |  |  |

Picklist: Balance b/d, Purchases, Purchase ledger control account, VAT, Purchase returns, Suspense.

A payment of £15,600 for computer equipment has incorrectly been entered in the accounting records as £16,500.

**(c)    Record the journal entries needed in the general ledger to remove the incorrect entry.**

| Account name | Amount £ | Debit ✓ | Credit ✓ |
|---|---|---|---|
|  |  |  |  |
|  |  |  |  |

**(d)    Record the journal entries needed in the general ledger to record the correct entry.**

| Account name | Amount £ | Debit ✓ | Credit ✓ |
|---|---|---|---|
|  |  |  |  |
|  |  |  |  |

## TASK 9                                                              (10 MARKS)

Kapoor's trial balance included a suspense account.   The journal entries to correct the bookkeeping errors, and a list of balances as they appear in the trial balance, are shown below.

**Journal entries**

| Account name | Debit £ | Credit £ |
|---|---|---|
| Suspense | 632 |  |
| Office expenses |  | 632 |
| Repairs | 873 |  |
| Suspense |  | 873 |
| Loan interest expense | 962 |  |
| Bank interest received |  | 962 |

**Account name**

| Account name | Debit £ | Credit £ |
|---|---|---|
| Office expenses | 8,420 |  |
| Repairs | 2,310 |  |
| Loan interest expense |  | 481 |
| Bank interest received | 481 |  |

**Complete the table below to show the new balances, and whether each will be a debit or a credit.**

| Account name | Balance £ | Debit ✓ | Credit ✓ |
|---|---|---|---|
| Office expenses | | | |
| Repairs | | | |
| Loan interest expense | | | |
| Bank interest received | | | |

## TASK 10 (14 MARKS)

On 31 March, Howard extracted an initial trial balance which did not balance, and a suspense account was opened. On 1 April journal entries were prepared to correct the errors that had been found and clear the suspense account. The list of balances in the initial trial balance and the journal entries to correct the errors are shown below.

Re-draft the trial balance by placing the figures in the debit or credit column. You should take into account the journal entries which will clear the suspense account.

| | Balances extracted on 31 March | Balances at 1 April | |
|---|---|---|---|
| | | Debit £ | Credit £ |
| Sales | 190,029 | | |
| Purchases | 104,698 | | |
| Admin expenses | 1,209 | | |
| Irrecoverable debt expense | 150 | | |
| Sales ledger control account | 28,200 | | |
| Discounts allowed | 4,090 | | |
| Purchases ledger control account | 28,929 | | |
| Bank interest paid | 300 | | |
| Bank loan | 16,700 | | |
| Fixtures and fittings | 43,000 | | |
| Computer equipment | 11,111 | | |
| Motor vehicles at cost | 4,567 | | |
| Motor expenses | 347 | | |
| Discounts received | 132 | | |
| Rent and rates | 1,678 | | |
| Light and heat | 980 | | |
| Suspense account (debit balance) | 35,460 | | |
| **Totals** | | | |

**Journal entries:**

| Account name | Debit £ | Credit £ |
|---|---|---|
| Sales ledger control account | 20,000 | |
| Suspense | | 20,000 |

| Account name | Debit £ | Credit £ |
|---|---|---|
| Bank loan | 15,460 | |
| Suspense | | 15,460 |

# Section 4

# MOCK ASSESSMENT ANSWERS

## TASK 1

**(a)**

| | True ✓ | False ✓ |
|---|---|---|
| A direct debit is an instruction to a customer's bank to make regular payments, which are usually of a fixed amount. | | ✓ |
| A cheque which is 7 months past the date of the cheque is considered to be 'out of date'. | ✓ | |
| The drawer of a cheque is the account holder who is making the payment. | ✓ | |

**(b)**

| | True ✓ | False ✓ |
|---|---|---|
| When Gates makes payments to suppliers by credit card, the amount paid effects the bank current account. | | ✓ |
| When Gates makes payments to suppliers by debit card, the amount paid affects the bank current account. | ✓ | |
| A cheque payment does not appear on the bank statement. | | ✓ |
| An unpresented cheque is a cheque payment that has cleared the bank prior to the reconciliation of the bank being performed. | | ✓ |

**(c)**

| Error in the general ledger | Error disclosed by the trial balance | Error NOT disclosed by the trial balance |
|---|---|---|
| Recording a bank payment for purchases on the debit side of both the bank and purchases account. | ✓ | |
| Recording a payment for rent and rates in a non-current assets account. | | ✓ |
| Recording a sales invoice in the sales account only. | ✓ | |
| Incorrectly calculating the balance brought down on the rent account. | ✓ | |

**(d)**

| Error | ✓ |
|---|---|
| Recording a bank payment for office expenses on the debit side of the office furniture account. | ✓ |
| Recording a payment for motor expenses in the bank account, motor expenses account and miscellaneous expenses account. | |
| Recording a payment by cheque to a credit supplier in the bank account and purchases ledger control account only. | |
| Recording a cash payment for travel expenses in the cash account only. | |

**TASK 2**

(i)

| Account name | Amount £ | Debit ✓ | Credit ✓ |
|---|---|---|---|
| Wages expense | 30,180 | ✓ | |
| Wages control | 30,180 | | ✓ |

(ii)

| Account name | Amount £ | Debit ✓ | Credit ✓ |
|---|---|---|---|
| Wages control | 10,311 | ✓ | |
| HM Revenue and Customs | 10,311 | | ✓ |

(iii)

| Account name | Amount £ | Debit ✓ | Credit ✓ |
|---|---|---|---|
| Wages control | 18,119 | ✓ | |
| Bank | 18,119 | | ✓ |

(iv)

| Account name | Amount £ | Debit ✓ | Credit ✓ |
|---|---|---|---|
| Wages control | 1,750 | ✓ | |
| Pension | 1,750 | | ✓ |

**TASK 3**

**(a)**

| Account name | Amount £ | Debit ✓ | Credit ✓ |
|---|---|---|---|
| Irrecoverable debt expense | 2,000 | ✓ | |
| VAT | 400 | ✓ | |
| Sales ledger control account | 2,400 | | ✓ |

**(b)**

| Account name | Amount £ | Debit ✓ | Credit ✓ |
|---|---|---|---|
| Cash at bank | 7,250 | ✓ | |
| Bank loan | 5,000 | | ✓ |
| Capital | 10,000 | | ✓ |
| Motor vehicles | 5,400 | ✓ | |
| Commission received | 575 | | ✓ |
| Stationery | 300 | ✓ | |
| Sundry expenses | 225 | ✓ | |
| Advertising | 1,000 | ✓ | |
| Rent and rates | 1,400 | ✓ | |
| **Journal to record the opening entries of new business** | | | |

**TASK 4**

**VAT control**

| Details | Amount £ | Details | Amount £ |
|---|---|---|---|
| Balance b/d | 16,750 | Sales | 46,750 |
| Purchases | 23,450 | Purchase returns | 230 |
| Discounts allowed | 870 | Cash sales | 3,450 |
| Petty cash | 70 | VAT refund | 6,430 |
| Irrecoverable debts | 640 | Office equipment sold | 1,230 |
| Balance c/d | 16,310 | | |
| | **58,090** | | **58,090** |
| | | Balance b/d | 16,310 |

The balance is owed to HM Revenue and Customs as a liability of £16,310.

**TASK 5**

**(a)**    **Purchase ledger control account**

| Details | Amount £ | Debit ✓ | Credit ✓ |
|---|---|---|---|
| Balance of payables at 1 May | 89,726 | | ✓ |
| Credit purchases | 62,362 | | ✓ |
| Cheque payments to payables | 87,251 | ✓ | |
| Discounts received | 11,928 | ✓ | |
| Returns outwards | 12,987 | ✓ | |

**(b)**    Balance b/d = Credit balance £39,922

**(c)**    **Reconciliation**

| | £ |
|---|---|
| Purchases ledger control account balance as at 1 June | 39,922 |
| Total of purchases ledger accounts as at 1 June | 51,850 |
| Difference | 11,928 |

**(d)**    Discounts received may have been omitted from the purchases ledger

**(e)**    Reconciliation of the purchases ledger control account assures managers that the amount showing as outstanding to suppliers is correct.

**TASK 6**

| Date | Details | Bank | Date | Cheque | Details | Bank |
|---|---|---|---|---|---|---|
| 01 April | Balance b/d | 18,000 | 01 April | 120045 | Mose Ltd | 6,234 |
| 19 April | Wallace | 5,321 | 01 April | 120046 | Sabre | 1,632 |
| 22 April | Bennett | 685 | 01 April | 120047 | Hannan | 41 |
| 22 April | Lewis | 282 | 02 April | 120048 | Flinderson | 4,444 |
| **4 April** | **Prince Paper** | **342** | 02 April | 120049 | Bratton | 542 |
| | | | 08 April | 120050 | Flax | 432 |
| | | | 08 April | 120051 | Vickers | 1,698 |
| | | | 14 April | | Staples | 2,878 |
| | | | **14 April** | | **Steamtown Mall** | **2,865** |
| | | | **22 April** | | **Bank charges** | **54** |
| | | | **23 April** | | **Overdraft fee** | **27** |
| | | | 24 April | | Balance c/d | 3,783 |
| | | 24,630 | | | | 24,630 |
| 24 April | Balance b/d | 3,783 | | | | |

**TASK 7**

(a)    Identify the details of TWO outstanding lodgements that should be entered into the bank reconciliation statement and show whether the amounts should be added or subtracted.

| Details | Amount £ | Add ✓ | Subtract ✓ |
|---|---|---|---|
| Packer Ltd | 1,206 | ✓ | |
| Miner Ltd | 1,725 | | |

(b)    Identify the details of TWO unpresented cheques that should be entered into the bank reconciliation statement and show whether the amounts should be added or subtracted.

| Details | Amount £ | Add ✓ | Subtract ✓ |
|---|---|---|---|
| D'Angelo | 410 | | ✓ |
| Klump | 275 | | |

(c)    Complete the bank reconciliation statement for Martinez Ltd for 30 June.

Bank reconciliation statement as at 30 June for Martinez Ltd.

| | |
|---|---|
| **Balance per bank statement** | £854 |
| **Outstanding lodgements** | |
| Name: Packer Ltd | £1,206 |
| Name: Miner Ltd | £1,725 |
| **Unpresented cheques** | |
| Name: D'Angelo | £410 |
| Name: Klump | £275 |
| **Balance as per cash book** | £3,100 |

(d)    Check that the bank reconciliation statement in (c) has been completed correctly by calculating:

•    The balance carried down in the cash book

•    The total of each of the cash book columns after the balance carried down has been recorded.

| Balance carried down £ | Cash book column totals £ |
|---|---|
| 3,100 | 11,431 |

**TASK 8**

**(a)**

| Account name | Amount £ | Debit ✓ | Credit ✓ |
|---|---|---|---|
| Suspense | 109,868 | ✓ | |

**(b)**   **(i)**

| Account name | Amount £ | Debit ✓ | Credit ✓ |
|---|---|---|---|
| Purchase ledger control account | 960 | ✓ | |

**(ii)**

| Account name | Amount £ | Debit ✓ | Credit ✓ |
|---|---|---|---|
| Purchase ledger control account | 9,600 | | ✓ |

**(iii)**

| Account name | Amount £ | Debit ✓ | Credit ✓ |
|---|---|---|---|
| Suspense | 8,640 | ✓ | |

**(c)**

| Account name | Amount £ | Debit ✓ | Credit ✓ |
|---|---|---|---|
| Bank | 16,500 | ✓ | |
| Computer equipment | 16,500 | | ✓ |

**(d)**

| Account name | Amount £ | Debit ✓ | Credit ✓ |
|---|---|---|---|
| Computer equipment | 15,600 | ✓ | |
| Bank | 15,600 | | ✓ |

**TASK 9**

| Account name | Balance £ | Debit ✓ | Credit ✓ |
|---|---|---|---|
| Office expenses | 7,788 | ✓ | |
| Repairs | 3,183 | ✓ | |
| Loan interest expense | 481 | ✓ | |
| Bank interest received | 481 | | ✓ |

**TASK 10**

| | Balances extracted on 31 March | Balances at 1 April | |
| --- | --- | --- | --- |
| | | Debit £ | Credit £ |
| Sales | 190,029 | | 190,029 |
| Purchases | 104,698 | 104,698 | |
| Admin expenses | 1,209 | 1,209 | |
| Irrecoverable debt expense | 150 | 150 | |
| Sales ledger control account | 28,200 | 48,200 | |
| Discounts allowed | 4,090 | 4,090 | |
| Purchases ledger control account | 28,929 | | 28,929 |
| Bank interest paid | 300 | 300 | |
| Bank loan | 16,700 | | 1,240 |
| Fixtures and fittings | 43,000 | 43,000 | |
| Computer equipment | 11,111 | 11,111 | |
| Motor vehicles at cost | 4,567 | 4,567 | |
| Motor expenses | 347 | 347 | |
| Discounts received | 132 | | 132 |
| Rent and rates | 1,678 | 1,678 | |
| Light and heat | 980 | 980 | |
| Suspense account (debit balance) | 35,460 | | |
| **Totals** | | **220,330** | **220,330** |